BORDER CROSSINGS

Marie-Louise von Franz, Honorary Patron

**Studies in Jungian Psychology
by Jungian Analysts**

Daryl Sharp, General Editor

BORDER CROSSINGS

A Psychological Perspective on
Carlos Castaneda's Path of Knowledge

DONALD LEE WILLIAMS

For Hilde Binswanger and Arnold Mindell

Canadian Cataloguing in Publication Data

Williams, Donald Lee, 1943-
  Border Crossings

(Studies in Jungian psychology; 8)

Bibliography: p.
Includes index.

ISBN 0-919123-07-4

1. Castaneda, Carlos—Allegory and symbolism.
2. Juan, Don, 1891-   3. Yaqui Indians—
Religion and mythology.   4. Jung, C. G. (Carl
Gustav), 1875-1961.   5. Psychoanalysis and folklore.
I. Title. II. Series.

E99.Y3W55   398′.15   C81-095004-9

INNER CITY BOOKS
Box 1271, Station Q, Toronto, Canada M4T 2P4

Honorary Patron: Marie-Louise von Franz.
Publisher and General Editor: Daryl Sharp.
Editorial Board: Fraser Boa, Daryl Sharp, Marion Woodman.

INNER CITY BOOKS was founded in 1980 to promote the understanding and practical application of the work of C. G. Jung.

Cover: Design taken from the surface of a "malacate," a baked clay spindle
wheel (*see page 14*) used in Mexico before the Spanish Conquest. This
figure and the several others here at the ends of chapters are from *Designs
from Pre-Columbian Mexico*, by Jorge Enciso (Dover Publications, New
York, 1971).

Glossary by Daryl Sharp.
Index by the author.

Printed and bound in Canada

Contents

Acknowledgements

I wish to acknowledge the years of help in working with the unconscious that I received from Dr. Arnold Mindell in Zurich, the profound insights into don Juan's world that he shared with me and the excitement about the path of knowledge that he generated during our work together.

I would also like to thank Maria-Chelaru Williams, Allen Ashby, Loren Wells, Linda W. Ferguson, Barbara Koontz, Jude Biggs, my analysands and the students at the C.G. Jung Center in Denver for their participation, stimulation and support throughout this work.

Introduction

In the summer of 1960, Carlos Castaneda, a graduate student in anthropology at the University of California at Los Angeles, met a "white-haired old Indian" named don Juan Matus, a *brujo* or sorcerer. Carlos Castaneda's pursuit of information from don Juan eventually became a pursuit of experience and authentic knowledge. Now, twenty years and five books later, Carlos is a fully fledged initiate into don Juan's "path of knowledge," and the account of his experience has found more readers than any other contemporary work in the psychological and spiritual tradition.

Clearly, Carlos Castaneda's remarkable apprenticeship to don Juan both enlivens and unsettles the Western imagination. Our psychological landscape has been touched and altered by Castaneda's stories, and it will continue to be touched for many years. His stories are fresh rain to our parched imaginations.

But despite the enormous fascination with Castaneda's work over the past twelve years, no one has examined the images of his experience in psychological detail.[1] What wounds of the psyche do those images offer to heal? To what infections, perhaps, do they make us vulnerable? How are we to understand the unfolding images of don Juan's world so that we may integrate his vision into our urban lives honorably and without shallow imitation? This book is an attempt to answer these questions.

Cardinal Points

We need to see, first of all, the context of our own lives, to see what we, like Carlos before us, bring to don Juan's Sonoran desert. That context, to begin with, is one in which the social and religious structures of the past no longer nourish us. We live in a spiritual vacuum.

For many people today, psychotherapy has replaced traditional religious, family, social and political solutions to life. The mainstream of psychology, however, does not address the needs of the spirit. The unconscious, when acknowledged at all, is generally seen as the troublesome container of repressed infantile and chaotic longings, rather than a creative factor offering the possibilities of meaning, direction and spiritual renewal. From most psychological perspectives our suffering is regarded as "nothing but" the consequence of the faulty mechanisms of consciousness. And this suffering is approached with an ever increasing variety of psychological techniques which may help to support the embattled and intimidated ego but which do not honor the deeper wounds or the deeper resources of the psyche. In consequence, our wonderful techniques impoverish the soul.

The psychedelic drugs of the sixties rushed into this spiritual vacuum. Although such drugs as LSD and mescalin showed us that the unconscious is more than the sum of our personal desires and conflicts, few people had the tools to understand their visions or to integrate them into the conscious framework of everyday life. Castaneda at least offered us images of integrating the unconscious material produced in altered states of consciousness. In the meantime, the initial value of psychedelic drugs anticipated in the 1960s was overturned during the 1970s in favor of their marketplace value and their ability, like alcohol and tobacco, to bolster and defend the ego's old ways rather than to create a new order.

The West also has witnessed a burgeoning interest in the religions of the East and the emergence of many groups formed around Eastern spiritual teachers; all offer to fill the vacuum. We remain largely unaware of an inner authority and of the unique resources of the unconscious, for it is both easy and tempting to project our inner authority onto a particular spiritual teacher or a religious tradition. Although this tendency may bring some genuine satisfaction and growth, it does not alter our original condition.

C.G. Jung, the one founder of modern psychology to make us aware that the unconscious actively produces meaningful symbols to compensate the loss of meaning we experience consciously, described shortly before his death the predicament of the modern individual:

> There are no longer any gods whom we can invoke to help us. The great religions of the world suffer from increasing anaemia, because the helpful numina have fled from the woods, rivers, mountains, and animals, and the God-men have disappeared underground into the unconscious.[2]

Each individual, therefore, has access to the healing activity of the unconscious psyche through dreams, fantasies, visions and other means. But we remain unnourished because of our conscious prejudices about the inner world:

> The Buddhist discards the world of unconscious fantasies as "distractions" and useless illusions; the Christian puts his Church and his Bible between himself and his unconscious; and the rationalist intellectual does not yet know that his consciousness is not his total psyche.[3]

Furthermore, writes Jung, Freud, who first opened the doors to the psyche and introduced us to the reality of unconscious processes, "inadvertently increased and confirmed the existing contempt for the psyche. Before him it [the unconscious] had been merely overlooked and neglected; now it has become a dump for moral refuse and a source of fear."[4]

Against this background, we find Carlos Castaneda writing about a Meso-American Indian shaman, don Juan, whom we can never meet. Castaneda is equally elusive; we have only the bare bones of a personal history for this man. Castaneda and don Juan have no cult and no following except among individual readers. In this way, Castaneda and don Juan are unique. We can struggle with the teachings of don Juan, and we can find ways through him to self-knowledge and to direct experience of the unconscious spirit, but we cannot find comfort or solace in a group of followers or in any way abdicate our own authority. The elusiveness of Castaneda is not a misfortune, but rather an offering.

Carlos Castaneda's apprenticeship to don Juan provides us with images of the process of turning to the unconscious for self-knowledge, for transformation and for an enduring relationship to the timeless realm of the psyche. Through Carlos's struggles to become a "man of knowledge," we glimpse what it means to be complete women and men and to grow beyond the confines of our personal and collective histories. If we persevere with him, we shall find that all of the old ideas about ourselves will be altered or shattered, and that we can no longer say we are "nothing but." Castaneda awakens in us the awareness of what it means to lead a symbolic life, and the ability to see deeply meaningful and powerful factors at work in the everydayness of our lives.

The first and most important point for Westerners is that Castaneda's teacher, the man who has fascinated the American public for over a decade, is an Indian. The spirit of the American Indian is the spirit native to this soil that would heal the wounds of the aged king, the old and worn attitudes that continue to rule us. At the same time, the Native American spirit is closer to us than the spirit of the East; it is the spirit of the land we inhabit and therefore more in harmony with our own unconscious roots. Not only is the Native American tradition our spiritual inheritance, the one we have virtually overlooked, but it is also a spirit that is capable of integration in a way the spirituality of the East is not.[5] Our psyches are more likely to be nourished by the dynamic individuality of the shaman than by the quietism characteristic of the East.

Jung observes in his essay on American psychology that the Indian is a numinous or "extraordinarily potent" factor in the psyche of the American, although a factor which largely functions without the direct awareness of the ego. He states that the Indian in the American's unconscious seems to be the carrier or symbol of heroic action and spiritual vision, and, I might add, of eros, a deep sense of relatedness to all life; the Indian appears wherever the American is at his or her best.[6] Jung also points out that the spirit of the conquered people, the Indians in our case, will inevitably get into the unconscious of the conquerors:

> Without conscious imitation the American unconsciously fills out the spectral outline of the Red Man's mind and temperament. There is nothing miraculous about this. It always has been so: the conqueror overcomes the old inhabitant in the body but succumbs to his spirit.[7]

It is time we reckoned with our host, and Carlos Castaneda has made one of the most serious attempts in our century at such a reckoning. Despite the attempts at revitalization within the Christian tradition, and attempts at attaining the transcendence of the spirituality of the East, I think the renewal that will take place within America will have its origin in the spirit of the Native American, even though we may not recognize the source.

Dramatis Personae

Carlos Castaneda introduces don Juan Matus as a Yaqui Indian shaman or sorcerer born in the Southwest in 1891. Don Juan was transported in 1900 with his father to central Mexico when the Mexican government exiled thousands of Sonoran Indians. He is said to have lived in central and southern Mexico from 1900 until 1940. Castaneda tells us that he met don Juan in Arizona in the summer of 1960 and that the apprenticeship was subsequently carried on in northern Mexico.

In 1968, Castaneda published his first book, *The Teachings of Don Juan,* describing a series of highly focused episodes from his experience as an apprentice to don Juan. In a tight 140 pages Castaneda covers the span of time from 1960 to 1965, beginning with his first meeting with don Juan in an Arizona bus station and ending with his frightening encounter with a sorceress and her attempt on his life. *The Teachings of Don Juan* concentrates mainly on Carlos's experience with three hallucinogenic plants: peyote (*Lophophora williamsii*), Jimson weed (*Datura inoxia*) and a mushroom (presumably *Psilocybe mexicana*).

Castaneda returned to Mexico in 1968, for the first time in more than two years, bringing with him a copy of that book. Though he had no intention of working further with don Juan, the visit proved to be the beginning of a new cycle of his apprenticeship. This new cycle is described in *A Separate Reality* and is concerned with Carlos's attempts through the use of the "little smoke" (*Psilocybe mexicana*) to *see* the mysterious background of everyday life. He struggled with the "guardian" of the other world and with the "ally," and was introduced to the deeper issues of sorcery beyond the superficial aspects of divination and power that concerned him throughout much of the first book. Also in *A Separate Reality,* we meet don Genaro, another sorcerer and ultimately Carlos's benefactor, the one who later initiates him into his most profound experiences of the unconscious.

The original manuscript of Castaneda's third book, *Journey to Ixtlan,* served as his dissertation for a Ph.D. in anthropology from the University of California at Los Angeles. In many ways this is the most sensitively written of all of Castaneda's books. It stems from Castaneda's review of his fieldnotes for *The Teachings of Don Juan.* Castaneda realizes that don Juan had begun introducing him to the sorcerer's description of the world from the first moment of their meeting, and that he had missed many of the most significant teachings of don Juan by directing his attention far too narrowly to the use of psychotropic plants. *Journey to Ixtlan* reveals the non-drug-related aspects of don Juan's teachings, from the moment of their first meeting until December, 1962. The last three chapters of the book jump ahead to 1971, and to Carlos's experience of the ally without the use of drugs.

Tales of Power appeared in 1974, and with this fourth book we find an enormous quickening of the pace of Carlos's acquisition of knowledge. By this time Carlos is capable of stopping his internal dialogue and of having direct access, without the use of drugs, to the unconscious, or to what don Juan calls the nagual, that for which there is no name. Don Genaro now enters a place of great prominence as Carlos's apprenticeship draws to a close. The book begins with Carlos's encounters with the ally and the double. It ends with a leap into the void, shamanic flight, and a final goodbye to his teacher and his benefactor. *Tales of Power* pulls together Carlos's apprenticeship as a comprehensible whole, and also provides us with a more carefully elaborated account of don Juan's theoretical framework for the path of knowledge.

In 1977 came *The Second Ring of Power.* It shows a dramatic break with Carlos's past as an apprentice. This book covers only the events of the few days of Carlos's first return to Mexico in two years since taking his leap at the end of *Tales of Power.* Now Carlos is a legitimate sorcerer. Don Juan and don Genaro are no longer available to Carlos. Nor are they available to us to make sense out of the chaos and confusion that arise when nine apprentices—five women (donna Soledad, Lidia, Josefina, Rosa, La Gorda) and four men (Carlos, Pablito, Nestor, Benigno)—come together with their strengths and weaknesses and their nine different points of view. These women and men face the task of continuing along the path of knowledge together and of working through their personal differences without a teacher to guide them. The reader of *The Second Ring of Power* is likely to be as baffled, troubled and disoriented as Carlos himself. After a brief but extraordinarily intense few days, Carlos leaves for Los Angeles. But he leaves with the knowledge that he will return, that this group of sorceresses and the sorcerers is bound together by fate, and that, furthermore, it is largely Carlos's task to lead them.

Don Juan: Fact or Fiction

Whether Castaneda's work is fact or fiction is a matter of legitimate interest. But the books attempting to establish Castaneda as a writer of fiction, such as Richard de Mille's *Castaneda's Journey* and *The Don Juan Papers,* direct too much attention to a question which is essentially a red herring. Far more important is the process of the path of knowledge as we see it unfold through don Juan, don Genaro, Carlos and the other apprentices. The degree of fact or fiction in Castaneda's work only becomes a serious issue when we are dealing with *The Second Ring of Power,* and I take up the question briefly in Chapter Six. Otherwise, whether don Juan is fact, fiction or a mixture of the two, he is quite real.

Carlos, on the other hand, is another matter. If we look at Carlos, making the distinction as de Mille does between "Castaneda," the author of the books, and "Carlos," the character in those books, we see that Carlos's attitude is highly routine and predictable—quite a contrast to that of don Juan.[8] This routine, predictable quality is more to be expected from a collective complex than from an actual sorcerer's apprentice; Carlos's routine behavior is, I think, largely fictional.[9] The Carlos of Castaneda's work seems to be the embodiment of old personal habits and collective tendencies, such as intellectualization, dependence upon reason, and fear of the unconscious. Carlos is a Western Everyman typifying our most familiar conscious routines. Carlos's *experiences* with don Juan have a feeling of authenticity. But his questions, explanations and concerns seem inauthentic, suggesting that he personifies a highly collective conscious attitude whose routines a nonfictional Castaneda would have recognized and disrupted relatively early in his work with don Juan. It appears that the fiction of Carlos's rational, analytic and suspicious conscious attitude was maintained throughout the first three books and gradually dropped in the last two books when it became no longer necessary or tenable.

Since I consider the Indian-ness of don Juan a significant aspect of Castaneda's offering, I need to mention one major and distinctively Indian value that is conspicuously absent in all of Castaneda's work. This is the value of community, of the ever-present concern for the well-being of the community. The absence may be understood as don Juan's shortcoming, or as Castaneda's narrowness of vision (which most of us share in this respect), or as an argument for the fictitiousness of don Juan. In any case, we in an industrialized society need to remain aware of the absence of the value of community, for this is a loss we collectively suffer from.

The apprentices of don Juan and don Genaro take up this task of supporting each other and shaping a community when they accept that they must learn to get along with each other. Perhaps in future books by Castaneda we will hear of their attempts to make a place for themselves in the everyday world.

The Approach

In the accounts of Carlos's experience in don Juan's world, we find a natural process of psychological evolution. Therefore, I have followed chronologically the images of Carlos's experiences as an apprentice and as a fully fledged initiate. Since I present the images themselves, the reader is not required to have prior acquaintance with Castaneda's work.

The broad outline of the process of inner development is visible in the division of this book. Chapter One examines the journey's point of departure and surveys the path and the goal. The apprentice to knowledge then strengthens his or her personality and builds a durable relationship to the unconscious by learning the ways of the hunter and the warrior (Chapters Two and Three). This process leads to detachment and to the further receptivity to the unconscious characteristic of the seer (Chapter Four). The apprentice then acquires the more thorough intellectual grasp of the structure of the psyche that is necessary for an adequate understanding of ecstatic or shamanic flight (Chapter Five). Following Carlos this far, we witness the introverted experience and realization of the unconscious. Up to this point, the inner vision has not been carried over into the life of the community. Now the extraverted aspects of the realization of knowledge begin to appear in Carlos's encounters with women and in the struggles of a small community of like-minded warriors (Chapter Six). Coming to the end of the material presently available, I close with the image of don Juan's and don Genaro's last gesture before leaving this world.

I approach Castaneda's material from a Jungian perspective because that is my particular standpoint and training. I amplify the images of Carlos's apprenticeship with comparative material from fairytales, myths, dreams and the literature of shamanic experience, and with references to the analytic process.

I frequently speak of "the unconscious." The unconscious refers, first of all, to everything we are not conscious of—all that was once conscious but has since been repressed or forgotten, and all that has never been conscious. The unconscious is a dynamic factor independent of our conscious intentions and wishes. It surprises and thwarts and often overwhelms us with emotions, inspirations, moods, slips of the tongue, dreams, fantasies, visions, neurotic symptoms, psychosomatic disturbances and so on. The unconscious acts upon consciousness through the above means in a way that seems purposeful. That is, the unconscious has in effect a consciousness of its own. Thus a product of the unconscious, such as a dream or psychosomatic symptom, points to a specific pattern or type of growth trying to occur in the individual. Finally, my use of the term unconscious is the equivalent in don Juan's vocabulary of the "other world," the "other side," the "nagual" and "magical time."

1

Beginning Images

It is the summer of 1961, a year since Carlos first met don Juan in an Arizona border town. Carlos has persistently asked don Juan to teach him about peyote. Don Juan has continued to avoid the topic. For Carlos, to learn means to gather information. For don Juan, to learn means to have direct experience. One more time Carlos asks don Juan to teach him about peyote, and once again don Juan refuses. Don Juan refuses because Carlos does not know his own heart.[10]

Where All Ladders Start[11]

Carlos, like most of us, approaches the path of knowledge with questionable goals, unexamined assumptions and little self-understanding. Carlos's psychology is worth examining because it dramatically colors the atmosphere and progress of his apprenticeship, and because we may find much of ourselves mirrored there: lack of self-esteem, preoccupation with power, fear of intimacy, preference for information over knowledge, inability to trust his own experience, extreme dependence on reason, and finally, ignorance of his own best qualities.

Carlos's low self-esteem makes its appearance in his first meeting with don Juan in the bus station. When don Juan is pointed out to him as an authority on peyote, Carlos makes a few awkward attempts at conversation and then impulsively begins to describe himself as very knowledgable about peyote and as a person worth getting to know. He would not go to such an extreme to justify his own worth if he did not have serious doubts about it. The impulsive, spontaneous attempt at self-enhancement, however, expresses a truth that Carlos is not yet able to acknowledge: he does know more than he is capable of admitting to himself. His exaggerated self-portrait exposes both his conscious sense of inadequacy and the larger, unconscious personality that is trying to emerge. Carlos's struggle with the demon of inadequacy is expressed in a number of ways: through his attempts to distinguish himself as an anthropologist, through his attempts to be special to don Juan, and especially in his concern with power and control.

The preoccupation with power and control is blatant in the opening pages of Castaneda's first book. We are introduced to don Juan's world with images of the power of witchcraft, of sorcerers who can transform themselves into animals, and with images of the uses of

15

"power plants." It is therefore no surprise that don Juan is shown to us more as a man to be feared than as a man to be loved and respected. Initially, the focus for Carlos is the acquisition of power, not self-knowledge. The destructive aspects of the power drive or complex are that self-knowledge takes second place to self-aggran-dizement and that relationships suffer from a lack of development.

I think it is because of Carlos's one-sided preoccupation with power that he ended the apprenticeship with don Juan at the end of 1965. Carlos's pursuit of knowledge and his relationship with don Juan were being suffocated. The apprenticeship could not continue without a change of attitude in the apprentice. This is precisely what we find happening in the spring of 1968 at the beginning of *A Separate Reality,* when Carlos renews his relationship with don Juan. Carlos visits don Juan to present him with a copy of *The Teachings of Don Juan.* With the quest for knowledge temporarily put aside, Carlos reconnects to don Juan through feelings of pleasure, warmth and affection. The experience of pleasure that Carlos has in don Juan's company becomes the basis finally for the renewal of the apprenticeship. Don Juan confirms that their work was disrupted because of Carlos's power complex when he says that Carlos quit because he "felt too damn important."[12] Power continues to be a major problem for Carlos throughout the apprenticeship, but it is less entrenched due to the interruption in his quest and due to his literary success.

C.G. Jung considered as opposites, not power and powerlessness, but power and eros:

> Where love reigns, there is no will to power; and where the will to power is paramount, love is lacking. The one is but the shadow of the other: the man who adopts the standpoint of Eros finds his compensa-tory opposite in the will to power, and that of the man who puts the accent on power is Eros.[13]

Carlos has adopted the standpoint of power; consequently, what is undeveloped and lacking for him is the experience of love and friendship. He will continue to struggle with the issues of relation-ship throughout his apprenticeship and beyond.

The power drive does have a positive side. As we have seen, it reflects a partial and compensatory truth to be integrated in the form of a legitimate sense of inner authority. It also behaves as a trickster, seducing Carlos into the attempt at knowledge. As with Carlos, ambitious power fantasies may stir up strong emotions that provide the energy necessary for great and difficult undertakings. We find an image for this process in an Eastern European creation myth where it is the devil who suggests to God the idea of creating the earth and humankind.[14] The devil in this instance is the equivalent of the power complex, the shadowy, inferior thing. In several versions of the myth, the devil is sent beneath the primordial waters to get the "seed of earth" for the creation. The myth is explicit, however, in identifying the creator: although the devil does much of the preliminary work (having the idea and fetching the first mud), the creative act itself can only take place in God's name. The power drive must give way to a higher purpose.

The other aspect of Carlos's psychology that colors his work with don Juan is his rationality. While reason is obviously a beneficial ally, Carlos carries it to an extreme. Indeed, he personifies the predicament of our time: the unyielding bias toward reason and the lack of consideration for feeling, intuition and the symbolic value of the subjective aspects of experience. Such dependence on reason may be an unconscious attempt at self-protection, but it ends by becoming a prison. Thus don Juan uses psychotropic plants with Carlos in an effort to shake up his assumptions.

The rational point of view allows one to dismiss the seemingly irrational aspects of experience as merely the effects of a drug. In this way the rationalist shields himself from the effects of the unconscious but fails to see the meaning of his experience. To the extent that this process prevails, the experience of the unconscious does not pass from the psychedelic to the psychological.

Like Carlos, we all have our reasons for approaching the path of knowledge, and our reasons are more than likely only shadows of some deeper urge. We approach the unconscious and begin to ask questions of ourselves because, most frequently, we wish to overcome a neurotic symptom or to save a relationship. We do not want to listen to our symptoms (depression, anxiety, sexual difficulties, stress, weight gain, etc.); we experience the unconscious as a problem to be solved rather than an invitation to live more deeply. Our symptoms are, however, precisely such an invitation, and they lead us to ourselves and to the greater mysteries in which we participate. Our symptoms may be a calling to the warrior's vocation.

The Warrior's Vocation

For the warrior on the path of knowledge, the first event in any series has symbolic value. When Carlos comes up to don Juan in the small Arizona bus station and begins "babbling inanities," don Juan considers the peculiarity of the event as an omen.[15] The odd conditions of their meeting, joined with the fact that don Juan *sees* something special about Carlos, leads him to suspect that Carlos may be a "chosen one." The most crucial omen or indication that

Carlos is "chosen" for knowledge comes when he takes peyote for the first time and is accepted by Mescalito, the spirit of peyote. As we shall see from examples of the omens that singled out the other apprentices, there are more common indicators of the warrior's vocation.

Traditionally, what signals an individual's calling to the path of knowledge is an unusual sickness with potent dreams or visions. Among the apprentices to don Juan, for instance, Josefina came to don Juan when she was crazy; Lidia was discovered alone, ill and prepared to die in an isolated mountain hut; La Gorda was overworked and overweight, and don Juan *saw* death hovering about her. Not everyone who falls ill or has powerful dreams is destined to become a shaman or shamaness. Election depends on the further beneficence of the unconscious, and on the capacity of the ego to contain the deeper experiences of the psyche. Election also depends on proper circumstances or conditions. For example, when Nestor and Benigno were struck by lightning, they were not alone; don Genaro, called by La Gorda a "thunderbolt sorcerer," was their witness. Finally, it is one's struggle with illness, suffering, and the demands of the unconscious psyche that allow one to touch sensitively the wounds of others.

Although it is not fashionable nowadays to speak of "a calling," the experience is quite common. A priest may tell, for instance, of an illness in youth and a religious vision at the time that determined for him the choice of the religious life. Someone else experiences and suffers from tremendous inner conflict that thrusts him at an early age into the world of psychology. A woman enters analysis to redeem a marriage and dreams at the beginning that an old woman takes her to the underworld to teach her ancient secrets; analysis in time becomes a "path with heart."

Frequently, the first dreams in analysis point to the nature of one's particular path of knowledge, the terrain it traverses, and how far it leads. Carlos, for instance, exaggerates his knowledge and his command when he meets don Juan, and once on the path he is always struggling to catch up with himself, to assume responsibility for the knowledge and the power he legitimately has. Pablito first met don Genaro when he literally ran into him while trying to slip away from underneath the booth in a city market, where he had been making love with the shop owner's daughter. Years later we see that Pablito's task as a warrior is tied to his relationships with women; he cannot slip away. His task is to let go of his mother, donna Soledad, to fulfill the claims of his manhood in a larger than sexual sense, and to establish relationships with the "little sisters" based on mutual respect.

In a number of instances, the omen says something about the relationship between the teacher and the apprentice. The two are often called to work together by a common task or wound. Don Genaro is drawn together with Nestor and Benigno through the encounter with lightning, symbolically the overwhelming power of illumination from above. We have already seen that Carlos has a problem with power. Don Juan was faced with the problem of power as a child, when the Yaqui wars brought death to his family and thrust upon him the conflict between the oppressors and the oppressed. Don Juan's awareness of the secret identity between power and powerlessness tips the balance in favor of understanding, affection and healing in the context of the common wound he shares with Carlos. We find the same motif in don Juan's first meeting with Lidia. While in the mountains he feels drawn toward a particular location; every time he turns away from that specific direction, the wind blows so stiffly that he can barely open his eyes. When don Juan finally finds Lidia in the rundown mountain hut, her eyes are infected and swollen shut. A common bond existed between them before they ever met.

The Enemies of Knowledge

Don Juan defines a man or woman of knowledge as anyone who has had the patience and the impeccability to follow the warrior's way, attempting to live in harmony with the unconscious and to follow the turns of his or her personal fate. In *The Teachings of Don Juan,* don Juan describes the four enemies of knowledge: fear, clarity, power and old age.[16] The second and third enemies are sought by the warrior and become enemies only after they have been acquired. We can regard fear in the same way, as an ally as well as an obstacle to be overcome. We need a fear of the unconscious, the same fear we would feel traveling treacherous waters. Fear informs us of danger and of possible consequences of action when we might otherwise go blindly and foolishly forward. Without fear there is no humanity, and those who approach the deeper layers of the unconscious without fear may well be swept away as madmen, eccentrics or inflated prophets. There is a Grimm fairytale about a young man who is disowned by his father because he does not know what fear is and who must go alone into the world to seek it.[17]

On the other hand, we must resist the tendency to succumb to and identify with our fear, to choose a temporary comfort over the distress of self-knowledge. We see people daily who have been challenged by something from the inner or the outer worlds and who, because they identify with their fear, have turned away from the encounter. We can mark the place on their path of knowledge where they have stopped, closed their eyes, run or set up obstacles to change. Don Juan suggests that the man who succumbs to this first enemy will turn into a timid, frightened man or a bully. The timid man identifies with his fear while the bully compensates for his fear with aggressiveness, projecting his cowardice onto his fellows.

As one pursues the path of knowledge in the face of fear, one comes to the second enemy, clarity. Since fear by nature puts one in a cramp and narrows consciousness, overcoming fear naturally expands the possibilities of conscious awareness and allows for more objectivity. The one who is taken by the second enemy will turn into a "buoyant warrior" or a "clown" who *sees* and laughs because nothing matters. The man who has identified with his clarity becomes intolerant of his own darkness and folly; he projects them onto his neighbors who become the objects of his laughter. The danger of clarity is that it is one-sided in favor of consciousness and the light principle, thereby depriving darkness of its legitimacy. To avoid succumbing to his clarity, the warrior must continually embrace his own darkness.

After countless struggles on the path of knowledge, the warrior gains power; witness, for example, the power of don Juan and his impeccable command of himself. To avoid claiming power is to live a partial life, but to identify with it is to succumb to the third enemy. Clinging to power creates a "cruel and capricious man," intolerant of weakness. The satisfactions of power blind him to his vulnerability and weakness. His weaknesses are projected onto his fellows whom he abuses in the same way that he abuses his own weaknesses, by denial or disdain. The man of power needs to be open to the vulnerability of the heart. The Huichol Indian shamans of Mexico recognize this fact and honor the need for a balance between power and vulnerability by using a chair made of strong *and weak* woods in all healing ceremonies.[18]

Although it seems that the fourth enemy, old age, is to be understood literally, we can also speak of it as a psychological attitude. Old age is a frame of mind we may fall into at any time. In its positive aspect old age is the wisdom symbolized by a lifetime of experience and introspection. This is the wisdom the warrior seeks. Yet it can also isolate him and deprive him of the rejuvenating energy of youthful visions. In its dangerous aspect this wisdom leads him to see everywhere the ceaseless interplay of the opposites; he feels that nothing new exists under the sun and becomes tired of the folly of his fellows.

To become a hunter, the average person must transcend fear. To become a warrior, the hunter must be willing to let go of clarity. To become a seer, the warrior must no longer care about power. Only when one has experienced the four enemies of knowledge, wrestled with them for their gifts, embraced them and let them go can one claim to be a man or woman of knowledge, and only then, don Juan says, at the moment of death.

The Average Man, the Hunter, the Warrior and the Seer

In describing to Carlos the differing relationships one may have to the unconscious, don Juan provides us with another fourfold typology of the development of consciousness.[19] An average man, he says, would be overcome by his fear if faced with a spirit animal alone in the forest. His fear would turn him into the prey of the unconscious. The average man has two possibilities; he can either run or take a stand against the animal. If he is not armed, he will run for his life; if he is armed, he will stop on the spot and drop to the ground.

The spirit animal don Juan refers to is a "magical deer," a manifestation of the psychopomp or guide who reveals the next step in one's process of individuation. Being alone in the forest is one situation in which powerful unconscious forces may emerge. Being alone, separated from one's environment, friends and routines, is equivalent to being stripped of one's shields against the unconscious. Marie-Louise von Franz, a Zurich analyst and long time collaborator of Jung's, remarks in *Shadow and Evil in Fairytales* that "loneliness invites the powers of the Beyond, either evil or good":

> The natural explanation would be that the amount of energy normally used in relating to one's surroundings is dammed back into oneself and activates the unconscious, loads up the unconscious part of the psyche, so that if for a long time one is alone, one's unconscious will come alive, and then you are caught for better or worse; either the devil will get you or you will find greater inner realization.[20]

The average man has two choices when the unconscious begins to break through his routine awareness. He may try to escape by flight, anxiously running from one activity to another, running to any place where for a moment a way seems clear, hoping always that this time things will be different. If, on the other hand, he is armed, he makes a stand; he uses whatever defense mechanisms are available (familiar from Freudian psychology) to drive off or kill (repress) the unconscious fantasies or impulses. In this case the personality is even further restricted, symbolized by freezing on the spot.

Despite the temptation to run from or to fall into the hands of the unconscious (as emotion, compelling fantasy, disturbing idea, impulsiveness, and so on), the hunter would make the unconscious his object of attention. A hunter is aware of the unconscious, and therefore in the isolation of the forest he looks for points of protection, places where the wind will not carry his scent. The hunter has developed an observing ego that he is capable of protecting under the most adverse circumstances. The hunter introverts and observes the mood or other form of unconscious libido. From this position he exercises his quickness of mind to comprehend what it is that the unconscious desires of him.

The warrior, in contrast to the average man and the hunter, directly goes to meet the challenge that has come his way. With his consciousness intact like a good hunter he uses "controlled abandon" to become one with the magical animal. The warrior deliberately reverses his conscious values in order to experience the other world, joins the object of his fear or longing in active imagination in order to know. The warrior not only observes the activity of the unconscious, he also participates in it through active imagination or other altered states of consciousness.

A person who travels the paths of sorcery finds no protection in the old ways he has left behind and consequently must adopt the way of the hunter or the warrior to withstand the frightening aspects of knowledge. The seer, on the other hand, does not have to approach the unconscious as a warrior. The seer anticipates the difficulties and dangers that the warrior meets face to face; the seer directs his life by what he *sees*. The seer has the capacity to *see* behind the surface of things, to know things "as they really are," and to grasp the seeds of the future. The seer is like the Taoist monk whose vision has detached his psychic energy from the thousand and one things of life. "Everything becomes nothing" for the seer and everywhere he *sees* the mysterious Tao.[21] The seer is receptive and fluid, whereas the warrior has a foot in two worlds and the alertness of one always close to death.

Four Visions of the Path of Knowledge

Don Juan and Carlos cross paths with several other apprentices who are in the mountains looking for power objects—quartz crystals.[22] Don Juan leaves them for a few minutes seated silently around a fire, their backs to the darkness. When don Juan suddenly reappears from behind a nearby boulder, the fire flares brightly and Carlos is shocked to find don Juan dressed as a pirate. When he again disappears behind the boulder, the men begin to discuss what they have just seen. Carlos learns that one of the other men saw not a pirate but rather a man wearing something like a black cowl and tunic, looking like a wild man who had perhaps just killed a friar and then put on the friar's clothing. Another of the young men disagrees and says that don Juan was dressed in rags and looked like a man returning from an "interminable journey." The third man saw don Juan as a wealthy and powerful rancher. These four visions may be seen as compensating the conscious attitudes of the four apprentices. Carlos, for instance, is timid, and his conscious hesitation is compensated by the aggressiveness of the pirate. Don Juan interprets his vision to mean that Carlos must learn to take what he wants from life. The attitude of the pirate would bring balance to Carlos, an introverted, intellectual man who feels that he does not deserve what he gets from life and certainly fears to take what he wants.

The image of the wild man who has murdered a friar suggests that the man who had this vision is a Spanish Catholic whose consciousness is dominated by collective Christian values. The wild and highly individual path of a shaman or sorcerer opposes and replaces the spirituality of the faithful believer. The image of the impoverished traveller would compensate the reality of an apprentice attached to the pleasures of this world, the warmth of a home and the traditions of the past. The path of knowledge will lead him far from home to the edges of his imagination and will strip him of his worldly attachments. The image of the wealthy rancher suggests an apprentice with an air of idealism and other-worldliness who must claim worldly power as a portion of his task of individuation.

The pirate, the wild man, the beggar and the wealthy rancher are all valid paths, just as are the intellectual, the Christian, the man of familiar comforts and the idealist. And although, as don Juan says, these paths all lead nowhere, yet any or all of them are worth following when they "have heart"[23] – that is, when it's where the energy wants to go.

The Method of Teaching

In *The Second Ring of Power* La Gorda tells Carlos how don Juan taught her and the other apprentices about consciousness and the unconscious.[24] Don Juan gathered a sack of everyday items and had the apprentices carry the sack and a table for miles into the mountains. Arriving at an isolated and distant place, don Juan set the table in the middle of a valley and arranged all the items from the sack on the table. He explained that the table and the items on it were like one's individual, conscious world. The unconscious, or nagual as he calls it, was the vastness of the valley that surrounded and supported the table. He then had the apprentices walk up into the mountains where they could look down on the table and the valley. He explained that sorcerers and sorceresses, unlike average men and women, must learn to view their own consciousness from a distant perspective. He then had the apprentices hike back down to the table and examine once more all the items on the table. While having them look away, don Juan removed various items from the table and then tested their memory to see if they could identify which items had been removed. They were all able to know what was missing from the table. Next, he cleared the table and had each person lie on his or her stomach across the table and scrutinize what was beneath the table. While having them turn away, don Juan removed several small rocks and branches from beneath the table. When asked to identify what was missing, the apprentices were as unsuccessful at this task as they were successful at the other. Finally, don Juan explained that the vastness of the mountains and the valley was too much for anyone to grasp, and consequently the area of the unconscious that a sorcerer or sorceress worked with was the area accessible to them, the area underneath the table or, we might say, the area in the shadow of the table. After this lesson about consciousness and the unconscious, the tonal and the nagual, the apprentices carried the sack and the table back out of the mountains.

A sorcerer or sorceress develops special attention for the table and everything on it, for all the elements of consciousness from personality to the external environment. By exercising this attention, the individual slowly but surely cleans and orders his or her conscious world. When this process of introspection and conscious action is underway, the apprentice learns to focus on what lies beneath the table, on what was once known but has since fallen out of consciousness, and on what has never been known or conscious. This is what don Juan calls the "second attention." At this point in the process of individual development one begins to approach one's totality, to experience both worlds, both attentions. One is no longer identified with the ego or the outer world nor with the unconscious, and thus one has the capacity for awareness of both worlds.

Don Juan understands learning as something inseparable from experience. When he introduces the apprentices to the tonal and the nagual, his words address the cognitive process (the tonal) and his actions address their unconscious perception via the body (the nagual). When they carry the table and the sack for long distances, their bodies learn and store the memory of what it is like to carry the burden of the familiar routines of consciousness. Then, bodily they experience the vastness of the unknown. The apprentices gain insight through don Juan's verbal communications and through reflection, while at the same time their bodies are also learning, making analogies and storing memories.

We, however, tend to separate the body from the classroom, the library, our talks with friends and our introverted deliberations; the body is not invited to participate.[25] An examination of the relationships between the body, the psyche and psychological complexes reveals the unnaturalness of this separation. Jung laid the empirical groundwork for a unified vision of the psyche and the body early in his career through his research on the nature of unconscious complexes. A complex is the image of an emotionally toned psychic process that "has a powerful inner coherence," is autonomous and subject to minimal control by the conscious mind, and is "incompatible with the habitual mode of consciousness."[26] He showed that every effect of an unconscious complex upon consciousness is accompanied by a physical event such as blushing, stuttering, a change in the breathing rate, muscular spasms, altered posture, etc. Complexes, Jung says, are the architects of dreams and symptoms.[27] By following the symbols produced in dreams or the physical disturbances produced in the body, one arrives at the complex. Arnold Mindell, a Jungian analyst practicing in Zurich, has carried this line of research further by giving the same attention to body processes in analysis as has been given to the symbolic processes at work in dream and fantasy life. Just as we speak of light as a wave or a particle, Mindell has shown that the same psychological process manifests in the two channels of psyche and body.[28]

Since the goal of don Juan's path of knowledge and of Jung's path of individuation is the "totality of oneself," the union of body and psyche is an integral part of the process of individual development. Turning now to the beginning stage of this process, we will examine how the hunter approaches this mythic task.

2

The Way of the Hunter

Don Juan and Carlos pause for a rest in the desert. After a period of silence, don Juan lifts his hat from his eyes, frowns at Carlos and says, "You have a knack for hunting. And that's what you should learn, hunting. We are not going to talk about plants anymore." Having arrived at this conclusion, don Juan immediately changes his tactic with Carlos. The same day he begins giving Carlos a detailed explanation of the behavior and routines of rattlesnakes. Next, don Juan manages to catch and kill a large rattlesnake which he then roasts for a meal. Don Juan urges Carlos to eat a portion of the snake and then gives him some pointers on what it means to be a hunter.[29]

Hunting as a Psychological Attitude

Don Juan's statements about hunting are a symbolic description of the psychological attitude appropriate for getting information from the unconscious. To begin with, don Juan tells Carlos that there will always be enough game for a hunter; a hunter can live off the land anywhere by hunting whatever game presents itself to him. In other words, if we are attentive, we can always find unconscious material to work with, whether at home, in a restaurant, at the office or alone in the desert. In the absence of dreams, fantasies or symptoms—the most obvious forms of unconscious material—there are other means of access to the unconscious such as gossip, slips of the tongue, bodily reactions, omens, synchronistic events, and all the features of our lives that are marked by repetition. Hunting is a daily affair, as the following two stories illustrate.

Not long ago, a man in his twenties came to see me for the first hour of analysis. He had just come from the university and we began with casual conversation about one of the professors, an excellent teacher who was losing his position because he had not published enough scholarly material. The young man identified with the professor, who was losing the "publish or perish" battle. Within a few minutes, he also mentioned that he was working in his spare time on a solar collector that could be used to run a Sterling cycle engine, and that the work was going very slowly. When I learned more about this man's life during the hour, it became clear that in our casual chatting at the beginning he had touched upon the core issues of his personal myth. He had been deserted by his father as a child and the loss hurt him in his capacity to value himself, his

26

creative instinct and his potential to have an effect in the world. Unconciously he knows he must produce something in his life or perish, and because of his lack of confidence he is afraid he will perish. A healing process, however, is occurring with the solar collector project in outer life. In order to produce something and get his engine running he must collect and focus his energy. When he is able to focus his energy, it will be available for effective use, symbolized by the Sterling engine. Building a solar (the father principle) collector, and transforming the sun's energy for use in the outer world, is identical with his inner psychological task: to consciously gather in or assimilate the father world, and then to act accordingly.

Virtually all the elements of his wounds and his potential for healing were contained in our first few minutes of casual conversation. Gossip was the hunting ground where we found the direction of his psychological process.

The other story involves a young man who asked me to exchange analytic hours for instruction in martial arts. We were discussing his idea over coffee in a nearby cafe. The conversation was becoming intellectual and arid when I noticed the young man repeatedly watching two women at a nearby table. He was obviously fascinated by one of the women, and I asked him what there was about her that caught his attention. He said that he was struck by the way the one woman listened and enjoyed the company of her friend, and I realized that just this element of relatedness was missing from our talk. I mentioned this to him, and he then began to talk more personally. This change of attitude rejuvenated the conversation.

Symbolically, we can say that the unconscious, something important of which he was unaware, was sitting at the next table trying to get his attention. In learning to hunt anytime, anyplace, we learn to observe the movements of the unconscious and to look for the meaning in its appearance.

A hunter accepts whatever the unconscious produces and works with that rather than holding onto the conscious designs and hopes of the ego. He or she does not hunt mountain lions when rabbits are in the field, nor pursue intellectual knowledge when feeling is called for. This receptive attitude is necessary because the unconscious is likely to confront us with something much different from what we expect. For instance, I worked with a woman who hiked into the mountains to be alone for two days to hunt for a vision. When she went to sleep, she hoped she would have a dream where she would "see the light." In her dream she did have a religious experience, but it was an experience of the darkness and not of the light. She dreamed that she was sucked inside the "world tree" and enveloped in a pulsating, warm darkness. The darkness was alive, and it was everything. In the roots of the tree, she found a small piece of wood on which was written all of world history. Although the dreamer was hunting for some enlightenment about her condition, she was asked by her dream to go deeper into darkness rather than pursue the clarity and differentiation that comes with solar consciousness. The dreamer, incidentally, was unfamiliar with the symbolism of the "world tree" and of the "tree book of fate" found in reports of shamanic experience.[30]

A hunter is not limited to a single view of the world, don Juan says. He can regard life from the point of view of his conscious ego as well as from the point of view of the timeless aspect of the psyche; he can consciously assess his situation, and he can see what the unconscious says through dreams and fantasies about the same situation. Unlike the hunter, most people are only vaguely aware of the possibility of hearing what the "Great Man" within has to say about life situations. As a child Jung experienced deeply these two complementary views of life:

> Somewhere deep in the background I always knew that I was two persons. One was the son of my parents, who went to school and was less intelligent, attentive, hard-working, decent, and clean than many other boys. The other was grown up—old, in fact—skeptical, mistrustful, remote from the world of men, but close to nature, the earth, the sun, the moon, the weather, all living creatures, and above all close to the night, to dreams, and to whatever "God" worked directly in him.[31]

The "Number Two" personality Jung described compensated the insecurities experienced by the ego, but to say this alone would be a grave distortion of the phenomenon. We all carry within us an "other" personality which connects us with all that is numinous and sacred, a world where time is not separated from timelessness. We commonly sacrifice the perspective of the Number Two personality as the conscious ego becomes more and more distinct. Although the sacrifice is to some extent natural and necessary in the evolution of consciousness, the denial of the timeless aspect of the psyche, when it persists, leaves us fragmented and incomplete. One must, according to Jung, "go forward—into study, moneymaking, responsibilities, entanglements, confusions, errors, submissions, defeats"—that is, into time—and yet not deny the perspective of the timeless and the sacred.[32] Similarly the hunter, don Juan says, lives in both time and timelessness.

Don Juan goes on to tell Carlos that hunters hunt because it is their nature to do so and not because they like it. To pursue the hidden life of the unconscious one must experience a calling; the choice of the vocation of a hunter is not a decision in the hands of the ego but rather a demand or offering from another source. The hunter-shaman's vocation makes its appearance, as we have seen, through omens, or through dreams and visions that occur spontaneously or as a result of a deliberate vision quest or intense suffering. Omens, dreams, visions and illness come to call the hunter-shaman, to reveal who he is. There is a deeper reason to hunt than any gratification it may offer the ego. Don Juan's words are cautionary: building a relationship to the unconscious becomes suspicious when it is too enjoyable, for then the gratification of the ego may take precedence over the ethical obligation to the object of one's hunt.

Next don Juan explains that a hunter must be in balance with the rest of the world and that otherwise hunting would become a meaningless chore. The hunting we are talking about becomes meaningless when it is carried out in a way that does not nourish the soul, that is, when it is done for ego purposes alone. There is no value, for instance, in working on our dreams only for the purpose of improving a relationship, or of overcoming anxiety and suffering, without acknowledging the implicit demands of the unconscious to live deeper and to know our suffering more fully.

Don Juan explains that he apologized to the rattlesnake for taking its life, knowing that one day death will come to him just so unexpectedly; the hunter, he says, is "on a par" with his prey. As symbolic hunters we thank the snake when we honor our dreams with respectful attention, take conscious responsibility for their meaning—the meat of the snake—and let the meaning live on in us. When we see that the same life force that produced the snake or dream requires something of us, then we have a balanced perspective. We balance the satisfaction of our hunger with an ethical or religious concern for the object of our hunt. Jung, too, speaks of the ethical relationship to the unconscious:

> It is equally a grave mistake to think that it is enough to gain some understanding of the images [of the unconscious] and that knowledge can here make a halt. Insight into them must be converted into an ethical obligation. Not to do so is to fall prey to the power principle, and this produces dangerous effects which are destructive not only to others but even to the knower. The images of the unconscious place a great responsibility upon a man. Failure to understand them, or a shirking of ethical responsibility, deprives him of his wholeness and imposes a painful fragmentariness on his life.[33]

The image of thanking the snake recalls a dream that was reported to a friend of mine by a young woman. In the dream the woman found herself in a dark cavern and she could see a light ahead toward which she began to walk. There was a smell in the cavern which she knew meant that snakes were present. As the dreamer got closer to the light, she saw snake women who told her not to be afraid as they were going to teach her their knowledge. After receiving instruction from the snake women, the dreamer knew that it was time for her to return home. The snake women were willing to show her the way out, but as a gesture of friendliness the young woman was obliged to kiss each of the snake women on the forehead.

We see in the dream the process we have been discussing of making peace with the unconscious and the same warning, that if she is not receptive to what she has been offered, she will not be able to find the way home. Since the snakes were feminine, and since snakes symbolize the deepest instinctive layers of the psyche, I would imagine that the dreamer was brought to the cavern, an introverted and archetypal place of transformation, because in her present life above ground she was out of touch with her feminine instincts. In its forward looking aspect, the dream indicates that the dreamer has the possibility of a connection to the deepest layers of the unconscious; from another perspective we might say that the dreamer is called to be a medicine woman.

There is one other aspect of the hunter's way I would like to mention. According to don Juan, "A hunter ... watches everything ... everything tells him some secret."[34] Thus far I have pointed out how the hunter watches for the appearance of the unconscious, but don Juan says that the hunter watches *everything*. The hunter looks into, around, beneath, behind and above things for their secrets. Since the hunter assumes that everything he needs is provided, he is not bored or disappointed; instead he wonders and watches. If he *is* bored or disappointed, he turns his attention to this feeling of emptiness and loss, and knows that in time this experience too will reveal something to him.

Attention is energy; attention warms things up. Therefore, in the process of being watchful, we incubate and the object of our gaze incubates; eventually a secret will hatch.

There are several obstacles to attaining this attitude. The first is that collectively we tend to assume that there is nothing more than what we see. In addition, we are too busy meeting deadlines, pursuing goals and satisfying the claims our possessions make upon us to watch. The states of being watchful and being in a hurry are to a degree mutually antagonistic. Another difficulty is that with our tendency toward specialization we depend more and more upon experts and fail to see our own resources. A man says to me, for instance, "I can't wait until someone offers a course on shamanism because I've been dreaming about medicine men," and I know that the problem is that he will wait when he should not wait; he should study the phenomenon, think, feel and imagine about it. But he will wait.

"Everything *tells* a secret," don Juan says. We may miss the secret because we are busily trying to fit what we have watched into the pattern of what we already know. If we can restrain the impulse to constrain the world to fit our description, we will be surprised to find the objects of our attention revealing something unexpected and new.

Finally, a major obstacle to the hunter's watchfulness is self-esteem. When our self-esteem is low, we are likely to assume that our lives, our feelings and thoughts and surroundings are not worth attention. Therefore, in learning to hunt we have to learn to care about ourselves.

I have been describing the hunter psychologically as a person with an individual, rather than collective, relationship to the sacred. As we shall see, this description is historically verified by the shamanic tradition found among hunting societies, in contrast to the priestly tradition associated with agrarian societies.

Shamans and Hunters

In *Primitive Mythology,* Joseph Campbell argues that the suppression of individualism is a major concern of the religions of agriculturally based societies, where "the lesson of the plants" is that the individual is "a mere cell or moment in a larger process."[35] By contrast, in the small groups of hunting and gathering societies there is an advantage in fostering individual endowment.[36] While hunting and gathering societies have their shamans like the agricultural societies have their priests, each hunter, unlike the planter, relies on shamanistic techniques and manages to care for personal, family and tribal needs with the aid of omens, dreams and frequently a spirit helper. The shaman's vision and power is individually determined, whereas the priest is a "socially initiated" member of "a recognized religious organization."[37]

The hunter-shaman is initiated through his experience of the unconscious rather than through a socially recognized religious body. One example is the account of the Siberian shaman Kyzlasov, who after extensive illness, visionary travel and instruction by ancestor spirits, presented himself to the ancestor shaman in a trance state for confirmation. The ancestor shaman measured the circumference, height and length of his drum, "counted the pendants hanging from it" and then presented him with helping spirits.[38]

The hunter-shaman is affirmed in his vocation by his inner experience, not by religious elders, universities or licensing boards. The hunter-shaman does undergo lengthy and rigorous training, but it is not orchestrated or supervised by a social body. Collectively we are experiencing ever increasing tension between the value of individual experience and endowment and the value of externally determined experience and training. In the field of psychology, for instance, there is a split between those who advocate stricter licensing requirements and those who would dismiss licensing requirements altogether and instead emphasize the integrity and depth of the individual's inner experience. The shaman and the priest are polar opposites. The shaman personality fails to see the significance of collective values, and the priest personality fails to see the value of unique inner experience.

In *The Flight of the Wild Gander*, Joseph Campbell retells an Apache myth that describes the tension between the hunter and the planter, the shaman and the priest. The myth originated during the period when the Jicarilla Apache, "originally a hunting people ... entered the area of the maize-growing Pueblos in the fourteenth century A.D. and assimilated the local neolithic ceremonial lore."[39] In the tale the Hactcin—Apache priests and counterparts of the Masked Gods of the Pueblo—were creators of the first world. In this world there were many shamans who began to talk and to quarrel about their powers. One spoke of stopping the sun overhead, another of getting rid of the moon. The Hactcin warned them about such talk, but it continued. On the fourth day the sun went through a hole in the sky, and the moon then followed—the first eclipse.

The Hactcin asked the shamans to use their power to bring back the sun and moon. Their display of power was impressive, but it failed to bring back the sun and moon. The animals were then given a chance, and they produced numerous gifts of nature but no sun, no moon. Then the Hactcin, the priests, began to act and out of their efforts came thunder, clouds, rain and rainbow. The Hactcin proceeded to plant seeds in four mounds of a sand painting. The birds and animals sang, and the mounds began to grow, eventually coming together to form one mountain. Twelve shamans were selected to become Tsanati, members of the dance society. Six Clowns were created and the Tsanati, Clowns and people joined in a dance to make the mountain grow. As the top of the mountain reached the hole in the sky where the sun and moon disappeared, four ladders were constructed so that everyone could ascend to the next world, our earth.[40] Campbell points out how the shamans were discredited, asserting that "the episode represents the victory of the principle of a socially anointed priesthood over the highly dangerous and unpredictable force of individual endowment."[41]

Such a conflict between the individual spirit and collective values is inevitable, but I think we will witness increased conflict and tension as the individual spirit becomes the more highly prized. In America, there is a tension between the rugged individualism which capitalism promotes as a value (and with which we as Americans are imbued), and the monopoly collectivism in which we actually live. I remember, for instance, returning after five years abroad and being struck by the television advertisements exuberantly proclaiming that "America loves..." or "America always relies on..." this or that particular product.

Jung labored to articulate a way between the two poles of collective identity and eccentricity, between submergence in social roles and grand isolation. He formulated the problem and challenge as follows: "Resistance to the organized mass can be effected only by the man who is as well organized in his individuality as the mass itself."[42] Through intense inner experience and reflection the individual, like the hunter we have been following, comes to know his or her unique path or myth. It is then incumbent upon the individual to avoid the seduction of "splendid isolation" and to relate to the collective through the uniqueness of that individual myth.

The young hunter who returns from a vision quest receives the new name by which he will be known from his visions. It is through his labor to live his vision faithfully that he finds his relationship to those he left behind when he sought himself in the wilderness. Campbell sees the possibility of our renewal in the archetype of the hunter-shaman:

> What is required of us all, spiritually as well as corporeally, is much more the fearless self-sufficiency of our shamanistic inheritance than the timorous piety of the priest-guided Neolithic. Those of us who never dared to be titans but only obedient children, following as loyally as possible the commands of Zeus, or Yahweh, or the State, now find that the commands themselves are in a somewhat fluent condition, changing with the time. For the circle has been broken—the mandala of truth.[43]

An example of the hunting way of life and its connection to shamanic experience is an Indian culture far removed from the Sonoran southwest—the Naskapi Indians of Labrador. It is clear from what we know that the Naskapi are hunters for food and hunters for the life of the soul. What the Naskapi hunt is the *Mista'peo*, the "Great Man" within. The Great Man has been translated as soul or ego; neither are quite satisfactory. It would be more accurate to see the *Mista'peo* as an archetypal image of the Self, the larger personality within, which is both personal and suprapersonal, human and divine, and which attempts to become actualized through us. The Great Man is located in the region of the heart—recall don Juan's "path of heart"—and is responsible for dreams:

> The Great Man reveals itself in dreams. Every individual has one, and in consequence has dreams. Those who respond to their dreams by giving them serious attention, by thinking about them, by trying to interpret their meaning in secret and testing out their truth, can cultivate deeper communication with the Great Man. He then favors such a person with more dreams, and these better in quality. The next obligation is for the individual to follow instructions given him in dreams, and to memorialize them in representations in art.[44]

This one brief paragraph about the Great Man summarizes the essential elements of the psychological attitude and experience of the hunter-shaman. The hunter pursues the Great Man; he hunts the unconconscious images that reveal to him who he is and what he is meant to be in his totality.

By paying respectful attention to these images, by attempting to understand them and by acting on the basis of our conclusions, we develop a closer relationship to the impersonal and objective center of the personality, the source of wisdom. Our efforts are rewarded by more and better dreams and hence by a deeper revelation of the richness of the psyche. And as we have seen before, we have an ethical responsibility to honor what we learn by living it.

Finally, there is one new element in the Naskapi description. That is the injunction to give creative expression to the sacred. The drawing below of a Naskapi hunter's Great Man makes it clear that the Great Man is an expression of wholeness and completion, that is, of psychic integration.[45]

The mandala formation of this image expresses through its fourfold and eightfold elements the differentiation of the personality. The balance of the elements in turn expresses the containment and the harmonious integration of the varied and contradictory aspects of the personality—light and dark, spiritual and earthbound, strong and vulnerable. The circular form protects the inner experience of multiplicity and unity, and of the rhythmic movement away from and into the center. Broadly speaking, we see in this mandala the creation of a central nucleus and the flowering of the whole personality.

People who follow their inner life, whether in or out of analysis, frequently experience the necessity to objectify a dream or vision through painting, sculpting or some other form of creative expression. Jung, for instance, painted or carved in stone representations of his inner experiences. Just as he painted mandalas before he realized their full significance, so too did Jung begin the construction of his Tower at Bollingen without knowing that it would be the "concretization" of his own individuation process.

> Gradually, through my scientific work, I was able to put my fantasies and the contents of the unconscious on a solid footing. Words and paper, however, did not seem real enough to me; something more was needed. I had to achieve a kind of representation in stone of my innermost thoughts and of the knowledge I had acquired. Or, to put it another way, I had to make a confession of faith in stone. That was the beginning of the "Tower," the house which I built for myself at Bollingen.[46]

> At Bollingen I am in the midst of my true life, I am most deeply myself.[47]

So far, I have spoken of hunting psychologically as a search for one's personal myth or meaning. Perhaps in this process we are also hunting for energy. If our conscious energy is at a low level, then we also turn to dreams, fantasies and active imagination to find an image of the unconscious content that is holding our energy. In *Creation Myths,* Marie-Louise von Franz has provided us with an interpretation of the dynamics of creativity. Here she describes the loss of energy so commonly associated with a creative mood or the emergence of some new content from the unconscious:

> In the individual case this is generally what we call an *abaissement du niveau mental,* which so often comes before an important content of the unconscious crosses the threshold of consciousness. This is partly an energetic phenomenon. Imagine that an important content, a big energetic load, is on its way up over the threshold of consciousness. When it approaches the ego complex it attracts libido from it, because, like mass particles, it has an effect upon the other particles, i.e., complexes; they affect each other like particles—and this content therefore attracts libido from the ego, causing it to feel low, tired, restless, depressed, until the content breaks through.[48]

In hunting the unconscious, we have to be prepared to change direction, to follow our hunches, to retrace our steps, to look for omens, to feel and follow up on the fluctuations of energy.

Frequently in analysis, a complex makes the analysis of dreams impossible, and one must first hunt and locate the conflict, the place where conscious energy is trapped. I am not referring to the situation where a person is in obvious crisis but to the more subtle moments when there is a feeling that something is wrong or missing. For instance, a person may bring up dreams and attempt to focus on them to avoid feelings for the analyst or to conceal a disturbing secret; it is necessary then to scrupulously hunt the genuine object of attention and source of emotion or energy. Or the work may appear to go well on the surface but be subject to the undermining influence of half-conscious emotionally toned assumptions. Such assumptions might be, "Yes, but my life will never *really* change," "This is interesting, but it's all just theory, and I can't take it too seriously," or "I'm sure you're not interested in me."

Analytic work teaches one to be acutely sensitive to the absence, presence and degree of energy in oneself and others. As von Franz points out, complexes attract energy, and becoming conscious of a complex releases energy. We will look now at the relationship between the hunter and the routines of unconscious complexes.

Hunters, Routines and Complexes

As Carlos is in the process of learning the routines of animals and the patterns he will need to know to be a good hunter, don Juan notices that Carlos is quickly making hunting a routine. Don Juan then unexpectedly makes a sound like a factory siren, proclaiming that it is lunch hour. Carlos stops building his trap for water rats and comes over to don Juan. Don Juan makes the noise again and says that unfortunately lunch seems to be over. Carlos goes back to his work on the cage. Don Juan makes the siren noise again in a few minutes and explains that it is five o'clock and time to leave; Carlos again drops his work. Don Juan has made Carlos aware of his propensity for routine. Now he can emphasize the idea that a good hunter must know the routines of his prey but that the hunter himself must have no routines.

The fact that don Juan imitates a factory whistle is significant: the major routine of Western culture is work. We work routinely, and we routinely turn any task or interest into work. Although the idea of analysis is to follow the unconscious, the work demon appears nonetheless, and then the game is lost. I think, for instance, of an analytic hour with a computer programmer who regularly overworked and who approached her problems as though they were program errors rather than opportunities to live more deeply. The hour had gone very well, but near the end she brought up a problem and became cramped with the need for an efficient solution. I felt her frustration, and struggled on for twenty minutes past the end of our appointment, although I had really wanted to end promptly in order to meet someone for dinner. When we stopped, it was with a feeling of dissatisfaction. The dissatisfaction naturally followed the narrow scope of our attention, the appearance of the work demon, and my consequent inattention to my own reality. I knew she needed to have more regard for her feelings and less for the puritan work ethic, but meanwhile I had ignored my own feelings and overworked. In short, I allowed myself to be eaten by our common demon and was of no help.

On the positive side, our routines protect us from the unconscious. They are shields against the unknown. We need to see, however, that as much as our routines protect us, they also lower the level of conscious awareness, alienate us further from the gifts of the unconscious and weaken our potential for authentic experience. What protects also weakens and finally harms.

Because our routines are by definition mechanical, they are easily recognizable: overwork, laziness, list-making, intellectualization, smoking, drinking, greed, ambition, seduction, caution—any form of behavior that reoccurs mechanically is probably a shield against some imagined or unimagined threat. Don Juan explains in *A Separate Reality* that a hunter or warrior learns to replace his routines with other shields, namely with all that is meaningful to him and touches the heart.[49] The true shield is the "path with heart."

The Plains Indians actually carried symbolic shields of hide on which were painted the individual's character, symbolic medicine and story as revealed to him through the vision quest. These symbolic paintings "told who the man was, what he sought to be, and what his loves, fears and dreams were. Almost everything about him was written there, reflected in the Mirror of his Shield.... The women also carried their Medicine Signs in ways to be seen, usually as symbolic designs woven with porcupine quills or beads on their dresses or belts."[50] Similarly, the only worthy shield for us is that of self-knowledge, the awareness of our personal myth.

One of the features of psychological complexes is that they are highly routine, just like the routine instinctive patterns of animal behavior. As Arnold Mindell pointed out in his Zurich lectures on don Juan, a hunter learns these routines by studying various behavior patterns. He learns about gods, goddesses, dwarves, elves, heroes, tricksters, water nixies, witches, fools, wise old men and women, and of course about the routines of one's family insofar as they show up subjectively as complexes. Jung too emphasized the importance of learning these routines—"the comparative anatomy of the psyche"—and insisted that his students study fairytales, mythology, comparative religion and primitive psychology because this collective material illustrates the archetypal patterns behind our personal conflicts.[51]

An archetype is not an inherited idea or esoteric image. Rather it is an instinctive, universal tendency to form certain ideas and images and to behave in certain symbolic ways. Archetypes, writes Jung, are *inner forces:*

> [They] spring from a deep source that is not made by consciousness and is not under its control. In the mythology of earlier times, these forces were called *mana,* or spirits, demons, and gods. They are as active today as they ever were. If they conform to our wishes, we call them happy hunches or impulses and pat ourselves on the back for being smart fellows. If they go against us, then we say that it is just bad luck, or that certain people are against us, or that the cause of our misfortunes must be pathological [a neurosis]. The one thing we refuse to admit is that we are dependent upon "powers" that are beyond our control.[52]

We cannot see the archetype or dynamic factor in itself, but we can recognize it through its representations and effects, just as we recognize the nesting instinct through the nest building behavior of birds.

One example of an archetypal routine is the hero. In *The Hero with a Thousand Faces,* Joseph Campbell shows us that the heroes of mythology vary immensely in their particularity, but nonetheless conform to a basic symbolic pattern of behavior common throughout the world (broadly speaking, a pattern of departure, initiation and trials, attainment of the "treasure hard to obtain," and return). Again and again, we see the details of the "hero's miraculous but humble birth, his early proof of superhuman strength, his rapid rise to prominence or power, his triumphant struggle with the forces of evil, his fallibility to the sin of pride (*hybris*), and his fall through betrayal or a 'heroic' sacrifice that ends in his death."[53] Because of our archetypal predisposition to form heroic images and to experience those images as having authority and numinosity, we can experience another person as heroic and speak of our own "hero worship." The other person's behavior does not exceed human limits, and yet because of the presence of the hero archetype we invest that person with god-like qualities. In this pattern of human response we can perceive the archetype in the background influencing our personal feeling and perception. Similarly, the archetypal image of the hero with all its numinosity is constellated in dreams and fantasies and when extreme situations confront us and demand that we give our utmost. Our heroic endeavors, our dreams and our idols, vary from person to person and from culture to culture but the heroic tendency itself is constant.

A fine illustration of the routines of a complex is the Grimm fairytale, "Jorinde and Joringel." It is worth retelling here:

There was once an old castle in a thick forest where an old woman lived alone. She was a witch, and during the day she took the form of a cat or an owl; in the evening she was again in human form. The witch could put spells on wild animals and birds, after which she would slaughter them and cook them for her meal. Also, any person who came within one hundred steps of the castle was forced by a spell to remain exactly where they were until she released the spell. When a young virgin came within the one hundred step radius, the witch would transform her into a bird and place her in a cage that she would then hang in the castle. She already had seven thousand such cages with rare birds.

One day a beautiful young virgin named Jorinde and the man to whom she was betrothed, Joringel, went for a walk in the forest. As the sun was going down they realized that they were lost. Inadvertently, they wandered within the one hundred step radius of the castle and fell under the witch's spell. When the witch appeared, she turned the girl into a bird in a cage like the others. But she had no use for Joringel and set him free.

Joringel was griefstricken and did not know what to do. He wandered until he came to a strange village where he took a job as a shepherd. During his free time he would go to the castle, taking care to stay out of range of the spell, but walking around and around the castle trying to think of a way to set Jorinde free.

One night he had a dream of finding a blood-red flower with a beautiful large pearl set in the middle. He took the flower, went to the castle and everything he touched with the flower was freed from the witch's spell. When he awoke from the dream, Joringel went into the mountains searching everywhere for such a flower. On the ninth day, early in the morning, he found a blood-red flower with a dewdrop at the center which looked like a pearl. He carried the flower day and night until he reached the castle, and when he stepped inside the boundary of the spell, he noticed that he was not affected. Upon touching the portal of the castle with the flower, the way was opened for him.

Joringel kept going deeper into the castle until he found the room with all the birds. The witch was there feeding the birds, and when she saw Joringel she spat poison and gall at him but could never come close to him. Joringel then touched the cages with the flower, freeing the birds, who were immediately transformed into their original shape and identity. He even touched the witch with the flower, destroying her ability to cast evil spells. Jorinde, beautiful as ever, threw her arms around Joringel, and together with the other young women they left the castle.[54]

The witch in this fairytale is the image of an autonomous negative complex capable of ensnaring young women's souls (or young men's souls, if we were to interpret the tale from a masculine point of view). The witch personifies the dynamic organizing factor—the archetype—at the core of the complex. The castle, on the other hand, suggests structure and order as well as rigidity, entrenchment and the idea that the complex itself is defended. A complex has a sphere of influence; as we get closer to it we fall under its spell. The extent of the influence of a complex (fifty steps or a hundred or five hundred) depends upon the intensity and frequency of the outside factor that constellates it, and upon an individual's ability or inability to deal with the accompanying conflict and suffering. For instance, if a mother abandons her child without explanation, both the child's relationship to women and his or her self-esteem will be more damaged than if the mother were merely separated from the child at intervals because of other obligations, while otherwise emotionally present and supportive. The intensity of the complex, however, depends not only on such observable personal facts but also on archetypal factors, in other words, on what the child's imagination does with the experience of loss.

Jung noticed that certain words will, by association, trigger a complex. The word association experiment that he developed early in his career is an accurate means of locating active complexes in the personality and assessing their intensity.[55] The test consists in the subject supplying responses to one hundred words that are read aloud by the examiner: for example, stimulus word "black," response "white," "water"—"land," "house"— ... (long pause) ... "strange." The disturbances created by the complex show up in emotionally laden responses, in the unusual nature of the response word, in a delayed reaction time, in a bodily reaction (gesture, blushing, fast breathing, etc.) or in some other observable form. The disturbance is the witch's spell.

Since the fairytale is about a witch, we should look at the routines of the negative mother complex. The witch behaves autonomously, spinning negative fantasies and feelings; the woman under her spell experiences guilt, hopelessness, fear of failure, isolation, anxiety. This complex may have solidified over many years, during which time the feelings and personality of the woman-as-child were denied expression, rejected as inappropriate or in some other way damaged. The power of the complex is increased when similar negating experiences occur in the world outside the family, and when the experience of unhealthy mothering is contaminated or aggravated by archetypal images of being devoured, thrown into the void, etc.

As soon as the woman risks herself and is vulnerable, the negative mother complex is constellated and the witch appears; the vulnerability is the child that constellates the negative parent either in the woman herself or in the environment as, for example, critical husband, friend, colleague. The stronger the emotion, the larger will be the complex's sphere of influence. Only a slight remark may trigger the complex and the woman is then convinced that the person across from her does not like her, that no one could ever like her. The woman, like Jorinde, is stuck in the spell of the witch, paralyzed with guilt and self-doubt. With this inner uncertainty, the woman responds to the environment in the only safe way she knows, by pleasing in a conventional way. At this point she is the bird in the cage.

In the fairytale, two things happen to bring about a solution, that is, to depotentiate the complex. The first is that Joringel spends a long time walking around the witch's castle; he observes the complex and suffers from it but avoids its spell. Joringel's behavior is equivalent to the psychological process of circumambulation: one circles the problem, examining it from every angle; the suffering is intensified and eventually warms and creates a deep awareness of the center. Joringel faithfully stays with the problem and allows a solution to incubate.

The other factor that contributes to the solution is Joringel's attention to the unconscious: he watches his dreams. Out of this concentration, the unconscious produces the healing symbol of the blood-red flower with the pearl at the center. The flower is symmetric; it is a mandala suggesting order in nature and symbolizing the balance and psychic integration lacking in the conscious situation. The passion of blood red is not antagonistic to the spirituality and purity of the pearl's whiteness; instead natural instinct is balanced by and able to be contained with purity of heart. Similarly, the transitory life of the flower and the enduring hardness of the pearl constitute a harmonious union of opposites, in Jung's term a true "symbol of transformation." The symbol expresses more in itself than we can apprehend with our consciousness, and its appearance produces effects. Whether this symbol in the fairytale heals the split between passion and love or the split between nature and spirit, it describes a condition of wholeness and produces freedom where there was once enslavement.

We have seen now that the hunter hunts for a deeper awareness of the unconscious complexes that affect him. In the process he carefully learns the routines of his complexes. Furthermore, he hunts for the direction, support and illumination of what the Naskapi call the Great Man and Jung calls the Self, the archetype of wholeness and the regulating center of the personality, the source of healing and transformation. Now we shall see that the routines of complexes are related, in don Juan's process of instruction, to what he calls being "accessible" or "inaccessible."

Accessible and Inaccessible

Having trapped five quail, don Juan lets three of them loose and roasts two for their meal on a barbeque pit lined with green branches. Carlos wanted to prepare all five quail. Don Juan tells him afterward that had they roasted all five, they might never have left the place alive. By this time twilight has arrived, the wind gotten cold, and don Juan sees the moment to teach Carlos about being inaccessible.

Standing on a nearby hilltop, don Juan has a "gesture" with Carlos about the power in the wind. A gesture is a highly instructive symbolic act. As they lie down and cover themselves with branches, the wind ceases to blow. As they make themselves noticeable by standing up, or by speaking, the wind searches and then comes. A "strong steady gust" hits Carlos's face, and he becomes unexpectedly terrified. At this point his body understands the gesture although his rational mind does not. The following day they stay around the house "on account of the wind"—another gesture—and don Juan tries once again to illustrate the need for being inaccessible. This time he focuses on Carlos's past relationship with a "blond girl," a "special person" whom he lost, don Juan says, because he made himself too accessible.[56]

Being too accessible, according to don Juan, is like being hungry, like squeezing out of shape, clinging, worrying. As most of our meetings with the world are tinged with, if not dominated by, hunger and greed of one sort or another, it is not difficult to find examples of this process. Collectively we are beset with one ecological catastrophe after another, the consequences of relating to the earth in a one-sided, power-oriented way. On a personal level, what we do to the earth and her response are comparable to what happens in many relationships. Just as we may deplete the earth by taking too much out of it, so we can exhaust a relationship by demanding too much from it—or putting too much into it.

The primary psychological factor involved in any relationship is projection. To the extent that we find in another person an unlived portion of our own soul and fate, we are attracted and driven to be with that person whether in love or hateful struggle. The other person may carry this projected aspect of ourselves for a time, especially when the projection is flattering or when it touches that person in a well-established complex (for instance, mother, father, inferiority, etc.). But projection always involves a weight on the other person, and eventually it exhausts and separates people as surely as it brought them together in the first place.

I once worked with a man who had fallen desperately in love with a married woman. She said she loved him but could not bring herself to leave her husband. He saw her as possessed by an insensitive husband, not strong enough to follow her feelings and come to him. He felt he had to use every opportunity to be with her because the time they had together was so limited. She was the sole interest in his life and he was naturally afraid of losing her. Since it did not occur to him to locate his own oppressed feelings, he was caught in a routine of desire and worry. She was the loved but unobtainable woman. The outer situation reflected his relationship to his inner life, his own soul: his own feelings were imprisoned, and in all of his dealings with life he had difficulty accepting responsibility for his heart. He pressured her to make a decision and grew weary, but he could not make a decision to get on with his own life.

One difficulty with recognizing projections is that they usually contain an element of truth. The woman, for instance, did lack the confidence and will to follow her heart. The feeling problem, therefore, was a common burden, but she alone was made to carry it, and the weight of that burden led to an end. A year later, she left both men to live on her own. If he had concentrated on his own feelings and interests in life rather than on pursuing and possessing her, his struggle might have freed her to follow him. Instead, exhaustion claimed the relationship.

Being inaccessible is not only or necessarily a matter of physical distance, which this couple had, but rather a conscious attitude, one that involves, in don Juan's words, "touching the world around you sparingly." Being inaccessible is tapping the other person lightly, not overloading him or her with our own psychology. It may mean at times being physically unavailable. When we find ourselves becoming all too available, we need then to inquire where the attraction or its opposite reflects something of our own that we have not yet realized, or to ask what question, yet unanswered, the other person poses to our own life. This is the process of withdrawing and integrating a projection; it releases energy and heightens the sense of individual integrity and freedom in a relationship.

Don Juan's description of the wind tallies with another aspect of projection. The wind is like a compelling, unconscious force that is beyond our control.[57] The wind, don Juan says, either "tumbles" or "twirls"; in other words, the wind either pushes and drives us or it spins and disorients us. When we are feeling driven or disoriented, then we can assume that we are too accessible and as hunters need to locate the source of the wind. Don Juan tells Carlos that there is a face in the wind; that is, whatever compelling force we are up against has a tendency to personify itself. The wind may be personified by a figure in dreams or fantasies, or by someone in the environment on whom an unconscious content is projected. The personification gives the wind an objective quality and provides us with specific information about itself.

In order to stay awake and travel during the night a hunter, according to don Juan, can deliberately make himself available to the wind, to a push from the unconscious. He can use the wind by moving in the same direction, for instance. When King Lear says, "Blow, winds, and crack your cheeks! rage! blow!" he is asking the wind, the wild emotion inside him, to push harder until he is able to *see*. The value of allowing oneself to be pushed is illustrated in the following dream of a young woman:

> I am in a town in the mountains with a man and we see that there is a flood coming. We begin to run for our lives, always managing to keep just ahead of the flood waters which rush toward our feet. While running we learn that my parents have been killed by the flood. Finally, we arrive at the highest point around, the top of the mountain nearest the town. The flood water is still just behind us, but it is no longer rising. On the other side of the mountain we see a beautiful and peaceful valley. The man turns to me and says, "This is your new life. Your parents are dead and now you have to take responsibility for your own life."

Outwardly the dreamer was very independent and controlled. Unconsciously she was bound to her parents, always wanting more from them than she received. If she were to follow the dream and let her emotions reach flood proportions (like seeking the push of the wind), her life would be changed. The old adaptation to life symbolized by her parents would die, and she would have the possibility of freely living her own life. The exceeding beauty of the valley that so impressed her seems to be an effort by the unconscious to draw her into the process.

Carlos's experience shows us that when the wind begins to blow, we can lie down and find that the wind, which was tumbling over us, is now caressing. We experience the tumbling when we are overwhelmed by our own or someone else's emotion, or for that matter by both simultaneously. I am reminded of an occasion when I turned over some official papers to a secretary and was vociferously attacked for some minor technical matter. She dramatically threw the papers in the wastebasket and then began to attack my character and my professional standing. In the past, I would have responded with an emotional defense or counterattack; this time I decided to "lie down." When she shouted that I was hopeless and could not do anything right, I remained quiet for a while and then told her that she was right, that no matter how hard I tried to do things correctly, my efforts never quite succeeded, and that I was indeed bothered and puzzled by my shortcomings. She immediately dropped her attack, picked the papers from the wastebasket and began to console me—the caressing wind. The true delight for me in this moment was the inner realization that if I could accept that I was hopeless, then I was free. My action brought a moment of illumination and that sense of liberation that comes, as don Juan says, when one considers that the worst has already happened.

A dream of my own amplifies this image of being inaccessible. It points to the inner spiritual dimension that takes one out of the "trafficked way." In the dream I was talking with my analyst on a summer evening. I remembered then two or three dreams that someone had asked me about, and I wanted to leave for a while to work on them. When I mentioned this intention to my analyst, he showed me the way to interpret the dreams. He lit a candle which he set on the ground, and then he lay down quietly on his back beside the candle. Today his gesture in the dream strikes me as the *not-doing* of dream interpretation. The candle attracts the meaning of the dream. It is the light of the heart with which the dream should be seen. As Jung remarked: "If our impressions are too distinct, we are held to the hour and minute of the present and have no way of knowing how our ancestral psyches listen to and understand the present."[58] When my analyst lay on his back in the dream, he was "saying" that the work of interpretation requires primarily a receptive attitude toward the dream images and toward the response of one's own psyche.[59] And it recalls that image of Carlos and don Juan lying on a hilltop, motionless and covered with branches, the wind changing from a "continuous gust" to a "mild vibration," sealing them in its power, protecting them like a cocoon.

Thus far we have discussed various aspects of the hunter's attitude toward life and the unconscious. We have seen how the hunter hunts. Now it is time to see that the one who hunts is also hunted.

Hunting and Being Hunted

Jung once remarked that his work on the unconscious was not just an experiment he was conducting but also an experiment being conducted on him.[60] Likewise, we are not only hunters but also the hunted. The archetype of wholeness, or the symbol of the New Man or New Woman, attempts to come into being through us, and when we are unwilling to go to meet our own totality, then we are likely to feel relentlessly pursued. More simply stated, we are hunted by the new life we resist and by the old conflicts we repress.

I am grateful to Allen Ashby, a poet and longtime friend, for the following three dreams of a woman. In the first dream, the woman was living in a cabin. A man approached and wanted in; she bolted the door to keep him out. In the next dream, a bear approached the cabin; the dreamer again bolted the door but more anxiously this time since the bear was more threatening than the man had been. In the last dream of the series, it was the devil herself (a woman in this dream) who asked to be let in; the dreamer pushed unsuccessfully against the door to keep it shut and woke up in a cold sweat.

We can see from these three dreams that something was trying to get through to the dreamer, that is, come to consciousness. Each time she closed the door to what asked for entry, the unconscious took on a more primitive and threatening form. The dreams show us that the more a complex, whether healthy or destructive, is repressed, the more likely it is to accumulate energy in the unconscious and so to threaten the conscious world with invasion. It is at this point that the hunter needs to be free of routines. To close the door is the routine reaction. To welcome and dialogue with who or what wants in is an act of freedom.

Although we are all hunted, it takes a particular form with creative and visionary personalities. From the literature of shamanism, for instance, we see that frequently individuals are called to the path of knowledge through great illness and suffering. The Huichol Indian shaman, Ramon Medina Silva, was singled out for his vocation by unusual dreams and by a snake bite at eight years of age that left him paralyzed for six months. He recovered from the illness knowing that it was his fate to become a "mara'akame" or shaman.[61] The Siberian Tungus shaman, Semyonov Semyon, explained that he was sick for an entire year before beginning to shamanize: "The sickness that forced me to this path showed itself in a swelling of my body and frequent spells of fainting. When I began to sing, however, the sickness usually disappeared."[62]

Another shaman from the Siberian region learned to engage in shamanic practices to cure his own illness. During the seven years in which his knowledge grew before he would attempt to cure others, he encountered in a vision a beautiful woman who was to become his *ayami* or helping spirit. Here is one of their dialogues:

She said: "I am the *ayami* of your ancestors, the shamans. I taught them shamaning. Now I am going to teach you. The old shamans have died off, and there is no one to heal people. You are to become a shaman."

Next she said: "I love you, I have no husband now, you will be my husband and I shall be a wife unto you. I shall give you assistant spirits. You are to heal with their aid, and I shall teach and help you myself. Food will come to us from the people."

I felt dismayed and tried to resist. Then she said: "If you will not obey me, so much the worse for you. I shall kill you."[63]

As the above examples show, the unconscious offers its gifts to the hunter but just as surely it makes unyielding claims.

The Magical Deer

Don Juan tells a story of the time after he had become proficient at hunting when, alone in the forest, he heard a "sweet whistle" that he knew belonged to no ordinary animal. He soon realized that he was in the presence of a magical deer. Since he knew that such a being would know the routines of hunters, don Juan did the unexpected thing: he stood on his head and began to wail and cry. When the deer approached, don Juan explained that he meant no harm. Then the deer soothed him and told him not to be sad.[64]

What is the nature of this deer? And what is to be made of don Juan's unusual manner of hunting?

The deer is a well-known representation of the archetype of the psychopomp or guide; in alchemical writings it appears in the guise of Mercurius (Mercury), sometimes referred to as the "fugitive stag."[65] Closer to home, we find that the Sacred Deer Person of the Huichol Indians of Mexico is also a guide and a messenger who carries the thoughts and feelings of the fire god, Tatewari, to men: "Tatewari reveals the messages and wishes of all the deities to the mara'akame [shaman], either directly in dreams and visions or indirectly through Kauyumari, the Sacred Deer Person."[66]

Kauyumari is a culture hero, guide, messenger and trickster. He "does not know himself" and "makes others crazy." But he is wise in his foolishness, and he reveals sense in nonsense. When the Huichol Indians journey to their sacred land, their place of origin, they hunt the Sacred Deer who will reveal to each a secret vision and perhaps the meaning of one's life. In the sacred land, the Sacred Deer takes the form of peyote, and the shaman actually stalks the peyote buttons, performs a ritual kill and, like all true hunters, insures through ritual treatment of the peyote that the Sacred Deer will live again. The magical animal don Juan hunts, therefore, is the elusive source of revelations from the "other side."

Judging from don Juan's behavior with the magical deer, we can say that it is the process of freeing oneself from the routines of personal and collective complexes that allows the deer, the symbol of the guide on the path of knowledge, to approach in a gentle rather than threatening manner. The deer approaches when, as the Chinese say about the sacred stag, "perfect rulers appear and the Tao of the king is accomplished."[67] In other words, we encounter the guide when we are in Tao, in the right attitude to life and nature.

Just as don Juan stands on his head, turning the world upside down, so he also wails although he is actually overjoyed with the possibility of an encounter with the magical deer. It is by turning things upside down that don Juan enters more into relation with the other world, the home of the spirit deer. Shamans often describe the World Tree in the underworld as being just the same as above earth, only reversed—one climbs down the tree to the nether world. There is often a shorthand way of finding out the position of the unconscious by looking at the reverse of the conscious attitude. If someone tells us that he would *hate* to trouble us, then we can infer that he would love to trouble us and will. Or the reversal follows of its own accord: "I don't want to interfere, *but* . . . "(Recall in this context the woman who wanted an experience of illumination and instead encountered primeval darkness.)

We find this same pattern of reversals enacted by the Huichol Indians on their pilgrimage each year to the sacred place where they hunt peyote with bow and arrow. The shaman Ramon Medina Silva describes this process: "On the peyote hunt, we change the names of things because when we cross over there, into Wirikuta, things are so sacred that all is reversed . . . everything should be upside down and backward."[68] Wirikuta, the sacred place, is the equivalent of paradise. The Huichols imagine this as "the opposite of the known world," and by consciously enacting reversals, Wirikuta becomes more vivid and tangible. The reversals bring the Huichols in harmony with the sacred world. The following passage gives some idea of what these reversals are like in practice:

> The camper became the "burro," who would stop "if he ran out of tequila" and who was traveling along a fine highway instead of the miserable ruts that passed as roads, and would eventually take us home "to Los Angeles." . . .
>
> The reversals applied to behaviors as much as to people and objects, thus one addressed someone in front of him by turning to the rear and one accepted something from another by telling him, "You are welcome," so that the giver replied, "Thank you."[69]

Don Juan enters sacred time and adapts himself to the deer with his reversals—standing upside down and weeping. Thus he balances the joy of a man about to find his life with the sadness of a man rendered lonely, foolish and perhaps even fearsome by his vision. Both the sadness and the joy are genuine. And perhaps it is the soul that, like the radiant deer when no longer threatened, whispers, "Don't be sad."

3

The Way of the Warrior

It is a night in August, 1961. Carlos joins don Juan and five other Indians to tap the other world through the use of peyote. Having chewed six peyote buttons and tasted tequila to take away the bitterness, Carlos becomes extremely thirsty. Don Juan brings in a saucepan of water and sets it on the floor. Carlos stares at the water that begins to look strange and glossy. He sees a black dog approach the pan and begin to drink. The dog becomes transparent, the water becomes iridescent. Carlos sees this iridescent water traveling through the dog and out the tips of the dog's hair, forming a "long white silky mane." The dog then becomes iridescent and light emanates from his body, "kindling him like a bonfire." Carlos drinks water from the pan just as the dog had done and perceives the same fluid running through his veins and passing like fibers out through the pores of his body. A sense of ecstasy begins to grow in Carlos, and he begins to play with the dog with complete abandon. He feels that the dog knows all of his wishes and that he knows the dog's wishes. Carlos is euphoric.

Later, as the effects of the peyote begin to wear off and he returns to his normal state of consciousness, he is horrified by the shift from the experience of euphoria with the dog to the sadness he experiences remembering that he is a man.

The next morning Carlos recounts the events of the evening. Don Juan interprets the experience, telling him that the dog he played with was Mescalito, the personification of the spirit of peyote, the inner guide along the path of knowledge. Mescalito, don Juan says, either accepts people or rejects them. He has seen Mescalito frolic, he has seen Mescalito make people laugh, but he has never seen Mescalito play with anyone. Don Juan interprets this unusual event as an omen that Carlos is a "chosen one," a person destined to follow the path of knowledge. Because of the omen with Mescalito, don Juan informs Carlos that he will teach him to become a warrior.[70]

Mescalito

Mescalito is a protector and a guide. One's experience of the unconscious through the use of peyote, therefore, is not a random experience but rather one that is organized and meaningful. Carlos's experience of the unconscious with peyote is guided and purposive, and Mescalito is the personification of the dynamic guidance of the unconscious.

49

Consciously, we tend to protect ourselves and to guide our lives through our philosophies, our moral principles, our common sense and our ability to think things through or feel things out. To some extent these conscious guides do work. Yet they often lead us into situations where we become hopelessly stuck. Then we need to hear from the unconscious.

Peyote is not the only means of finding guides outside our consciousness. We can encounter the unconscious through emotions, moods, fantasies, dreams, omens, physical symptoms, synchronistic events, or perhaps through divinatory practices (tarot, the I Ching, dice, etc.). By examining all or some of these various manifestations of the unconscious, we can become aware of what is in effect a consciousness in the unconscious, symbolized here by Mescalito, a source of wisdom that is beyond the bounds of our usual conscious resources and of far greater depth.

During one sequence in *A Separate Reality,* don Juan recommends peyote to his nephew Lucio and to Lucio's friends.[71] Lucio and the others protest that they have their own protectors—Christ, Mary and the Virgin of Guadalupe. Don Juan argues that their protectors have not helped them to live a proper life. Their defense is that Christ, Mary and the Virgin of Guadalupe could help if only people would listen to them. Don Juan responds that Mescalito is a protector of a different order because Mescalito forces one to listen.

The symbols we turn to for guidance, whether Christ or Buddha, fail to make us listen when they have lost their numinosity or their connection to the living waters of the unconscious. Through centuries of conscious reflection and elaboration on our religious symbols —Christ, Mary, Abraham, Moses, Buddha and so on—our consciousness has usurped the place of religious experience. Thus for many people, ideals of proper conduct associated with our religious symbols have replaced religious experience. Don Juan's talk with Lucio and his friends exposes the problem of many modern individuals who find that the familiar symbols have lost their vitality. They no longer have the potency to guide us through the entanglements of present-day ethical conflicts. It is for this reason that one turns to the unconscious for enlivenment, a sense of direction and the possibility of transformation.

The split between conscious and unconscious values (here between Christ and Mescalito) has historical antecedents. It shows up, for instance, in the conflict between the Church and the alchemists. Although most medieval alchemists considered themselves Christians, they were nonetheless in conflict with the traditional values of Rome because they recognized a guiding principle other than Christ.

This guiding principle was personified in the figure of Mercurius.

There are some striking symbolic parallels between Mescalito and Mercurius. For instance, Carlos experiences Mescalito as radiating a fiery light and at the same time as iridescent flowing water. Mercurius is called the "divine water," "the water that does not make the hands wet."[72] At the same time, Mercurius is fire, the "secret, infernal fire, the wonder of the world, the system of the higher powers in the lower," and "the universal and scintillating fire of the light of nature, which carries the heavenly spirit within it."[73]

In later experiences with Mescalito, Carlos again encounters the fire and the water. He is carried over strange waters and then sees Mescalito whose eyes are made of the same water. Water appears universally as a symbol of the unconscious psyche, and thus, we can say that through Mescalito Carlos sees things from the eyes (or consciousness) of the unconscious, of nature and the timeless psyche. In his next experience, Mescalito appears as a brilliant shaft of light that illuminates both earth and sky. Here Mescalito is the light of nature (plant life, peyote), the divine spark of the spirit present in earthly nature.

Mescalito, like Mercurius, is unpredictable because the opposites are united and present in him, and because one never knows which of his aspects the god will reveal. Speaking for Mercurius the alchemist says, "My water and fire destroy and put together."[74] Mescalito can be deadly or playful, merciless or healing. The following quotation from the *Rosarium*, a medieval alchemical text, provides a clear sense of the dual nature of this archetype of the guide:

> By the philosophers I am named Mercurius; my spouse is the [philosophic] gold; I am the old dragon, found everywhere on the globe of the earth, father and mother, young and old, very strong and very weak, death and resurrection, visible and invisible, hard and soft; I descend into the earth and ascend to the heavens, I am the highest and the lowest, the lightest and the heaviest; often the order of nature is reversed in me, as regards colour, number, weight and measure; I contain the light of nature; I am dark and light; I come forth from heaven and earth; I am known and yet do not exist at all; by virtue of the sun's rays all colours shine in me, and all metals. I am the carbuncle of the sun, the most noble purified earth, through which you may change copper, iron, tin and lead into gold.[75]

Both Mescalito and Mercurius are compensatory to the consciousness of the Western world, which is dominated by the Judeo-Christian tradition. Christ is the light of revelation and is a symbol of the wholeness of the psyche, but over the centuries all that is dark and hints of evil has been repressed or excluded from the collective understanding of this symbol of the God-man. Mescalito and Mercurius, on the other hand, are light but also close to darkness, high but also low, life but also death. Jung says of Mercurius in this regard:

> In comparison with the purity and unity of the Christ symbol, Mercurius . . . is ambiguous, dark, paradoxical, and thoroughly pagan. It therefore represents a part of the psyche which was certainly not moulded by Christianity and can on no account be expressed by the symbol 'Christ.'[76]

There is a parallel to the Mercurius-Christ relationship in Mexican mythology, where Quetzalcoatl (the Nahuatl god of consciousness) is compensated in the unconscious by Tezcatlipoca, a god of darkness and of the processes of nature. Tezcatlipoca, Mescalito, Mercurius and Kauyumari (the Sacred Deer-Person) all compensate the predictable, structured routines of consciousness and bring one to an experience that is spontaneous, natural and highly individual. They provide a rite of passage into our own individual myth. But there are dangers involved.

Don Juan tells Carlos that if Lucio had approached Mescalito with his characteristic greed, Mescalito would have destroyed him. The Huichol Indians express this same idea in regard to Kauyumari when they speak of the "other peyote": "That other peyote, that which one buys, it did not reveal itself in the Huichol manner. One did not hunt it properly, one did not make offerings to it over there [in the sacred land]. That is why it is not good for us."[77] The Huichols also speak of two kinds of peyote that look very much alike, good peyote (*Lophophora williamsii*) and bad peyote (*Ariocarpus retusus*). One is more likely to eat the bad peyote, called *tsuwiri*, when one has not approached the god in a sacred manner:

> If one comes there not having spoken of one's life, if one comes not having been cleansed of everything, then this false *hikuri* [peyote] will discover it. It is going to bring out that which is evil in one, that which frightens one. It knows all one's bad thoughts.[78]

In other words, the face we show to the unconscious is mirrored by the face the unconscious reveals to us. As the alchemists said of Mercurius's behavior: "Good with the good, evil with the evil."[79]

Let us now look at how the unconscious guides Carlos through his experience of peyote. His experience includes a difficulty in speaking, the perception of luminous water and the playful interaction with a dog. First of all, speaking detracts from the immediacy of experience for Carlos; talk is one of the conscious tools he uses throughout his apprenticeship to avoid the unconscious. Therefore the first thing Mescalito does is to close off this avenue of avoidance. Carlos is pushed to stay with his own inner experience rather than being allowed to dilute it by talking.

In Mescalito's first act with Carlos there is a message for many of us, because we have a strong tendency to shy away from the experience of ourselves as we really are by immediately talking *about* and not *with* what we feel. Oddly enough, the tendency to shy away is often exacerbated in America by the emphasis on "relating." This emphasis leads us to attend so much to the other person that we sacrifice our own experience. The unconscious frequently compensates this conscious tendency with autonomous behavior that leads away from contact, behavior such as avoiding eye contact, closing the eyes, coldness, and yawning. In therapy it may be unwise to interpet such behavior as resistance; often it is a spontaneous attempt to sustain feeling for oneself or to go deeper into one's own experience rather than risk losing it by trying to relate.

Carlos's perception of the luminous flowing water and his playful interaction with Mescalito call attention to the fluidity he needs in his everyday life. Mescalito guides Carlos away from his rigidity and opens him to playfulness, spontaneity and the warmth of instinctive contact. The problem that Mescalito speaks to is the despair that Carlos awakes with. Mescalito guides Carlos to an experience of the pleasure and fulfillment he lacks consciously.

Once don Juan sees that Mescalito has singled Carlos out as a "chosen one," he begins to introduce Carlos to the more difficult challenges of knowledge. He attempts to shake loose some of Carlos's routines through the use of the devil's weed and secondly, the little smoke.

The Devil's Weed

Near the end of August, 1961, don Juan introduces Carlos to the devil's weed (Jimson Weed).[80] He calls the devil's weed a feminine ally who leads a man to power. The various parts of the weed may be used respectively to cure illness, to make people crazy, to restore vitality, to increase endurance, to stir up passion or to practice divination. Only one portion of the devil's weed, the seeds, strengthens the heart; the other three portions serve the various goals of power.

As we saw with Mescalito and peyote, there is a psychic factor projected onto the devil's weed. The particular nature of the altered state of consciousness produced by the devil's weed invites the projection of a feminine figure by men and of a masculine figure by women. For Carlos, therefore, the devil's weed is somewhat like a woman. For a woman, the devil's weed would behave rather like a man.

Jung called these archetypal complexes the anima and the animus. On the basis of a general or archetypal human tendency and on the basis of early experience, we all form quite unconsciously an image of the opposite sex. The anima is the image of woman in a man's psychology, and the animus is the image of man in a woman's psychology. We all have experience of the devil's weed or of the anima/animus. But we normally remain unconscious of the experience because we exercise little objectivity about our moods, emotions, opinions and inspirations that actually originate with this inner "other" of the opposite sex.

How are we caught in the entanglements of the devil's weed and how may we tame her/him as an ally?

Let us first examine the experience of the anima. Imagine a man who meets a woman at a party. There is something about the way she looks and talks and moves that fascinates him. He approaches her with excitement but also some fear. They only have a chance to talk briefly, but for days afterward he cannot get her image out of his mind. It feels like he has always known her; perhaps he thinks she is a genuine soul-mate. He has met the anima, the devil's weed. Something about the woman has invited the projection of the man's image of what a woman is, and because he knows so little about her, there is nothing to set up a resistance to the projection.

Meanwhile the woman may be projecting her own animus image onto the man. Later will come the involvement and the subsequent clash between image and reality. If they survive the disappointments and frustrations, a conscious relationship may develop; or they may separate, being disappointed that the other person is not who they thought they were. The image the man projects has a personality of its own, and that personality affects his consciousness in specific ways. If he is a good hunter or warrior, he will recognize that personality as it affects him in dreams, through his emotions and fantasies and through the women he may project this image onto. The same process holds true for women with the image of the animus.

Let us imagine another common experience of this projected image. A woman has a stormy relationship with a man. She finds him creative and interesting but eternally irresponsible, irritatingly aloof at the wrong moments, and perhaps unfaithful. Hurt and angered once too often, she tells him to leave. She is troubled by the fact that in all her relationships with men over the past few years, the pattern has been the same. The faces, names and personal habits have been different, but each man has been exciting but distant, creative but irresponsible. Each relationship has begun, proceeded and ended in much the same way. The image she has of a man, the animus or devil's weed, has involved her through the power of projection with these men and has structured her experience of the relationship. Perhaps she dreams of responsible but boring business-men, and interesting but irresponsible artists, and has some difficulty being responsible to herself and her own creative drive.

We experience the anima/animus not only in projected form. The image we carry of the other sex also appears in dreams. And these images stand behind our unexamined emotions, moods, opinions, inspirations, plots, fantasies and so on. Examining these various manifestations of the unconscious leads to self-knowledge and to an awareness of the deeper mysteries of life. This process of examination and evaluation is what don Juan calls taming an ally.

Before one can reach the seeds of the devil's weed, however, one must struggle with all of the dangerous aspects of this psychological process. The anima and animus, writes Jung, "are deceptive phantasms compounded of supreme sense and the most pernicious non-sense, a veritable veil of Maya which lures and leads every mortal astray."[81] And don Juan says the devil's weed is seductive, cunning, shifty and "hard with her proteges," continually testing the limits of one's understanding and fiber. The complex personified by the devil's weed whispers of our unrecognized greatness and later reminds us that we will never amount to anything. When we are in a "devil-ish" mood or affect, the weed has us. The weed insists that we be perfect and dwells on our imperfections. It seduces us and entangles us with sexuality and ambition and creative urges. Objectivity is not a characteristic of the first three portions or "heads" of the devil's weed. In fact, the words, "always" and "never" often signal the presence of the anima or animus: "You're *always* busy when I ask you to do something!" or "You'll *never* grow up!" We are seduced by the devil's weed into identifying completely with our emotions, opinions and fantasies, but by personifying the weed or the anima/animus, we can grasp the autonomous nature of this complex and comprehend its true intent or purpose.

The devil's weed complex is personified by Castaneda on another occasion as an "entity of the night" that seduces one off one's path with melodious sounds.[82] While walking in the mountains at night, don Juan goes considerably ahead of Carlos, and Carlos has to stay on don Juan's trail by listening to and following don Juan's imitation of an owl cry. The distinctive mark of don Juan's imitation is that it is "raspy" at first and then mellow. The "entities of the night," however, make "very melodious sounds" and have difficulty imitating the raspy cries of a man or of an actual bird. As Carlos follows he begins to hear sweet sounding owl cries to his left. A dark mass crosses in front of him, and he hears another more compelling owl cry, one so gentle that it calms his fear and tempts him to stop. At this moment he hears don Juan's raspy cries, and he rushes on.

Just so may the anima lure a man off course. Carlos, as we have seen, is lured off the path by his depression, his feelings of worthlessness, his self-doubt. Von Franz describes this negative aspect of the anima in *Man and His Symbols:*

> In its individual manifestation the character of a man's anima is as a rule shaped by his mother. If he feels that his mother had a negative influence on him, his anima will often express itself in irritable, depressed moods, uncertainty, insecurity, and touchiness.... These "anima moods" cause a sort of dullness, a fear of disease, of impotence, or of accidents. The whole of life takes on a sad and oppressive aspect. Such dark moods can even lure a man to suicide, in which case the anima becomes a death demon.[83]

In *The Odyssey,* the Sirens behave like "entities of the night" and would lure Odysseus off course. Odysseus has himself tied to the mast and has his crewmen plug their ears so that the sweet music of the Sirens will not tempt them to shore. Odysseus is forewarned, like Carlos, about the dark side of the unconscious, about the alluring beauty of darkness, about the darkness of seemingly innocent beauty:

> Square in your ship's path are Seirenes, crying
> beauty to bewitch men coasting by;
> woe to the innocent who hears that sound!
> He will not see his lady nor his children
> in joy, crowding about him, home from sea;
> the Seirenes will sing his mind away
> on their sweet meadow lolling. There are bones
> of dead men rotting in a pile beside them
> and flayed skins shrivel around the pot.[84]

One's secret strength when faced with the deadly aspects of the anima/animus is one's attachment to everyday life—Odysseus to his home and family, Carlos to his affection for don Juan's "raspy" humanity. In fact, the lure of the unconscious often has the effect of strengthening one's conscious standpoint. Out of fear we compensate the pull of the devil's weed by affirming the values of the heart, by clarifying who we are. The "virility" that one needs in dealing with the devil's weed is the strength of conviction about one's authentic identity.

The warrior goes further in his relations with the anima than the hunter does, by entering into dialogue with her in active imagination. Jung describes this process and its effects in *Memories, Dreams, Reflections:*

It is she [the anima] who communicates the images of the unconscious to the conscious mind, and that is what I chiefly valued her for. For decades I always turned to the anima when I felt that my emotional behavior was disturbed, and that something had been constellated in the unconscious. I would then ask the anima: "Now what are you up to? What do you see? I should like to know." After some resistance she regularly produced an image. As soon as the image was there, the unrest of these emotions was transformed into interest in and curiosity about the images she communicated to me, for I had to try to understand them as best I could, just like a dream.[85]

In this way, one is able to grasp unconscious processes when they are still in the "seed" form and have not yet taken roo.. Consciousness is then able to extract what is meaningful and valuable from the activity of the anima/animus and participate more completely and wisely in the unfolding of events.[86] Thus one "tames" the "fourth head" of the devil's weed.

In making an ally of the devil's weed, it is important not to rigidify the contrasexual aspect of this complex. It is tempting to generalize, to say that a man's anima complex will have an affective quality (emotional, moody) because men tend to imagine women as more emotional, and that a woman's animus will have an abstract quality (opinions, ideas) because women tend to imagine men as more rational. This approach, however, breaks down for two reasons: one, because individuals are specific rather than general, and two, because the qualities we imagine to be feminine or masculine do not have universal validity but rather exist as trends (and obsolete trends, at that) in our own culture, in our own time. There may have been a time, when we were closer to our biological roots, that individuals conformed to specific sexual traits that were easily recognizable as masculine or feminine. And men and women will continue to experience each other as different and will continue to experience that difference as something fascinating and troublesome, regardless of the particular nature of the difference. Though our images may change, they will remain a constant psychological factor to be dealt with as the anima, the animus or the devil's weed. But it is no longer possible to assign particular traits to the masculine or the feminine principle, or to men or women, with the stamp of absolute truth. In the process of individuation we are called upon to realize ourselves as individuals, that is, to trust and follow our own unique experience regardless of whether or not it matches the general trend.

The dreams of two contrasting women illustrate this approach. The first woman is receptive to the impressions she receives from her environment. She is sensitive to the feelings of others, and it is

important to her to sustain an atmosphere of warmth in her relationships. She dreams, however, of making friends with an aggressive
man who seems to know what he wants in life and to be single-
minded about his intentions. She is attracted to him but afraid of
him. What is trying to develop in this woman is an attitude that
would give more definiteness to her personality and that would
allow her, when necessary, to pursue her own ends despite the
damage it may cause to the harmonious atmosphere she has created.
Whereas her conscious attitude is more diffuse and receptive, the
unconscious animus attitude that is trying to emerge is focused and
direct. This is the nature of the ally she needs to tame.

The second woman is an active, highly effective professional
woman in a position of leadership. She is sensitive to the feelings of
others but directs her relationships far differently than does the first
woman. In her dream she discovers an upstairs room in her house
that she did not know existed. There is a large window with the sun
pouring in on shelves of exotic plants. The walls are covered with
paintings and sketches. Curled up in a chair in the corner is a young
man absorbed with a poem he is writing. His mind is far away, and
he does not notice her entrance. Here the animus suggests to the
dreamer an attitude far different from her own, an attitude that
wants to be incorporated as an integral part of her life. The man's
consciousness is organic, aesthetic, dreamy and drawn to intangibles.
What this woman experiences as the masculine principle is for her,
at this time in her life, dreamy.

Though our images may vary enormously, we all experience the
other sex and our image of the other sex as in some way different
from ourselves. The differences are not absolute. Indeed, I suggest
that we dream up differences ultimately to become conscious, since
only through the tension of differences do we become conscious.
The devil's weed may seduce us into the entanglements of life or
seduce us out of life, but if we attend to her/him, she/he will make
us conscious.

The Little Smoke

After being introduced to the devil's weed, Carlos is told about don
Juan's other ally, the little smoke.[87] The little smoke opens the
apprentice to his capacity for psychic objectivity because the nature
of this hallucinogenic mushroom produces a state of dispassionate
clarity.

Jung experienced the same psychic factor that is personified by
the little smoke when he encountered a figure named Philemon in
active imagination. Philemon was an old man with the wings of a

kingfisher, the horns of a bull and four keys which he held as if he were about to open a lock. Through his inner dialogues with Philemon, Jung came to understand the profound objective reality of the psyche.

> In my fantasies I held conversations with him, and he said things which I had not consciously thought. For I observed clearly that it was he who spoke, not I. He said I treated thoughts as if I generated them myself, but in his view thoughts were like animals in the forest, or people in a room, or birds in the air, and added, "If you should see people in a room, you would not think that you had made those people, or that you were responsible for them."[88]

Similarly, the little smoke brings to the apprentice the objectivity lacking in his or her experience of the devil's weed.

The little smoke is ingested with the use of a pipe, and from don Juan's handling of the pipe it is clear that the pipe is as symbolically significant as the little smoke itself. The pipe is the physical symbol of the relationship a man or woman develops between the ego and the unconscious; it is a bridge, a peacemaker, a symbol of relationship and of the principle of eros. The eros aspect of the pipe and the objectivity of the little smoke are intimately connected. In analysis, for instance, the faithfulness of the analyst's objectivity may offer the most profound acceptance of one's full individuality. This kind of deeply respectful objectivity is often the most loving act one individual may offer another. Such objectivity is uncontaminated and clear and yet at the same time intimate and binding. On this deep level, objectivity (the little smoke) and eros (the pipe) are one.

We find an exceptional elaboration of the symbol of the pipe and the smoke among the Sioux Indians. The gift of the pipe was brought to the Sioux by a woman of the other world, the Sacred Buffalo Calf Woman. The pipe not only relates the Sioux to the world of the spirit but also to their fellow men and women, to the earth and to all of creation. Joseph Epes Brown describes the ritual use of the pipe:

> In filling a pipe, all space (represented by the offerings to the powers of the six directions) and all things (represented by the grains of tobacco) are contracted within a single point (the bowl or heart of the pipe), so that the pipe contains, or really *is*, the universe. But since the pipe is the universe, it is also man, and the one who fills a pipe should identify himself with it, thus not only establishing the center of the universe, but also his own center; he so "expands" that the six directions of space are actually brought within himself. It is by this "expansion" that a man ceases to be a part, a fragment, and becomes whole or holy; he shatters the illusion of separateness.[89]

The pipe establishes peace between opposing parties—between the ego and the unconscious, oneself and one's enemies, heaven and earth, spirit and matter, mind and body.

In our Western heritage we lack such rituals for establishing a relationship with the unconscious and with the objective earth and its inhabitants. Once the "word" was our bridge to the mysteries that unite us. That relationship between the word and the pipe became clear to me several years ago. In 1976, I had to fly to Washington on personal business, and at the end of my last day there, with nothing left to do, something pulled me a last time into the Capitol where, beneath the dome, my eyes wandered to the four emblems carved in stone above the archways, emblems of our relations with the Indians. One in particular struck me: a settler holds a scroll that reads "TREATY" while an Indian extends a pipe. I saw that the pipe and the printed word are equivalents; they are both sacred objects.

While the Indian's relationship to the spirit is carried by the pipe (an eros principle), it is the word (a logos principle) that carries that relationship for us. Unlike the Indian, however, we have no living ritual by which to sanctify our words. Our words no longer transport us into sacred time and no longer reconnect us to our own center or to the center of all creation as the pipe has done for the Indian. Jung speaks of this problem in "The Undiscovered Self":

> Far too little attention has been paid to the fact that, for all our irreligiousness, the distinguishing mark of the Christian epoch, its highest achievement, has become the congenital vice of our age: *the supremacy of the word,* of the Logos, which stands for the central figure of our Christian faith. The word has literally become our god and so it has remained, even if we know of Christianity only from hearsay. Words like "Society" and "State" are so concretized that they are almost personified. . . .
>
> No one seems to notice that this worship of the word, which was necessary at a certain phase of man's mental development, has a perilous shadow side. That is to say, the moment the word, as a result of centuries of education, attains universal validity, it severs its original connection with the divine Person. There is then a personified Church, a personified State; belief in the word becomes credulity, and the word itself an infernal slogan capable of any deception. With credulity come propaganda and advertising to dupe the citizen with political jobbery and compromises, and the lie reaches proportions never known before in the history of the world.
>
> Thus the word, originally announcing the unity of all men and their union in the figure of the one great Man, has in our day become a source of suspicion and distrust of all against all.[90]

Perhaps we may be fortunate enough to see the time when the spirit of the Native American, as eros, will unite the land and heal our wounds. Then, perhaps, a symbol may emerge as potent and sacred as the word once was.

La Catalina

The perplexing episode of Carlos's struggle with the sorceress named La Catalina, in *The Teachings of Don Juan*, is thematically and psychologically related to his struggle with the devil's weed.[91] The fact that La Catalina is referred to in each of the other four books (though she never reappears) indicates that Carlos is still fixated on the power complex she represents.

One day Carlos arrives and finds don Juan with a broken ankle. Don Juan explains that the broken ankle is no accident; he was pushed by a sorceress, La Catalina, who is out to kill him. Carlos asks if don Juan will use witchcraft to stop her. The question betrays Carlos's standpoint, his interest in power and magic. On another visit to don Juan, Carlos finds him extremely disturbed because La Catalina had appeared again in don Juan's house in the form of a blackbird. Don Juan explains that he woke up just in time to fight for his life, and at this point tells Carlos that he is his trump card. Carlos can save don Juan from death by surprising La Catalina himself. Out of compassion for don Juan, Carlos agrees to take on this "worthy opponent." In subsequent episodes, Carlos has several frightening and bizarre encounters with La Catalina that leave him fearful for his life. At the end of *The Teachings of Don Juan*, Carlos has one last "battle of power" with La Catalina. He is successful, but by this time the experiences of the devil's weed, the little smoke and La Catalina have been so disturbing that he decides to end the apprenticeship.

Throughout these episodes La Catalina is described as a witch or sorceress. She is not mentioned as a seer but rather as a powerful witch, a master of magic. As we have seen, the devil's weed teaches one about power: sexual power, vigor, adventuresomeness, the ability to manipulate others. Carlos was seduced by the power of the weed, and we know from *Tales of Power* that Carlos was attracted to La Catalina and virtually drooled when he saw her. Carlos was also seduced into testing his power with La Catalina, again an effect of the devil's weed.

To round out the story of Carlos's battle with La Catalina (and psychologically with the devil's weed), we need the additional information don Juan provides when he recapitulates for Carlos the course of the apprenticeship and clarifies his strategy as a teacher.[92] Don Juan was never threatened by La Catalina; he invented the story in order to trick Carlos into fighting with her, because Carlos was at the stage where it was tempting to withdraw from the path of knowledge.

Don Juan employed the strategy of finding Carlos an opponent in order to force Carlos to test and use everything he had learned in the apprenticeship, and to insure that out of necessity Carlos would continue to learn. Don Juan explains that there is a time when most people would choose the ordinary life over the difficult path of the warrior, and that the teacher must see to it that the apprentice chooses the impeccability of a warrior. The opponent, then, is someone who would force the apprentice to live like a warrior in order to survive.

In the episodes with La Catalina and in Carlos's struggle with the devil's weed the task is the same—to rise above the seductions of power. Although don Juan from the beginning disavows any interest in power or in the devil's weed, he nonetheless falls prey at times to the power principle. For instance, we can examine don Juan's invention of the story of La Catalina's threat to his life as a story that expresses a symbolic truth. By trapping Carlos, don Juan himself succumbs for a time to the third enemy of knowledge, power. What seems to be the most crucial decision on the path of knowledge is taken from the apprentice and placed in the hands of the teacher. How, we may ask, does the teacher know that he is not robbing the apprentice of his fate? Don Juan's trap is an attempt to coerce or manipulate (third "head" of the weed) Carlos in a particular direction. Not only does it betray a lack of trust in Carlos but also a lack of trust in the unconscious, something otherwise most unlike don Juan.

Don Juan's contention that a trick is necessary to keep someone on the path of knowledge is disturbing. As don Juan himself later points out, in *Tales of Power,* the most important decisions in life are really in the hands of the nagual or the unconscious. Nature, not the teacher, provides the trick to keep us growing. If one thinks to turn back from knowledge, outer circumstances may conspire like fate to close the door to the past, making it impossible to return to the exclusivity of one world. Or illness may drive one back to the path of knowledge, as commonly occurs when a shaman gives up his fatiguing profession, then falls sick and only recovers when he begins to shamanize once more. Dreams may insist on the choice. Finally, the successful choice of impeccability and the life of a warrior is meaningful only when one can also fail to make that choice.

Looking at don Juan's story about La Catalina sneaking up on him while he was asleep, we see that the story is true on a symbolic level. The power principle threatens don Juan when he is unconscious (asleep, napping) of his own plotting. Don Juan is tripped up and loses his standpoint as a result of the power complex. Nowhere in Castaneda's work is don Juan more unconscious of his use of power than when he tricks Carlos.

We can also look at the symbolic meaning in Carlos being don Juan's trump card. Carlos can help because he is largely the source of the problem. Carlos stirs up the power complex by projecting all the power onto don Juan. The projection occurs as follows: Carlos is unconscious of his tendency to control all of his meetings with don Juan and his encounters with the unconscious. Instead of being shocked by his own manipulative behavior, Carlos continually projects his manipulative, controlling tendencies onto don Juan. He frequently imagines that don Juan has somehow gotten friends together to trick him, and he theorizes that the experiences with peyote are mostly the result of "the manipulation of social cues."[93]

With the exception of the La Catalina episode, don Juan is normally not manipulative, deceitful or power driven. By continually resisting the knowledge he is there to seek, however, Carlos is always inviting don Juan to assume a power position. As Adolf Guggenbuhl-Craig says in *Power in the Helping Professions,* "The patient's sorcerer-and-apprentice fantasies have a very powerful effect on the therapist, in whose unconscious the figure of the magician or savior begins to be constellated."[94] Carlos's desire to learn is projected onto don Juan; he then resists don Juan and thereby invites don Juan to force him to learn. With this idea in mind, it is understandable that don Juan would imagine Carlos could save him from La Catalina— Carlos rescues both of them from the power complex by struggling with it himself rather than projecting it onto don Juan.

In order to deal with the frightening aspects of knowledge symbolized by the devil's weed, the apprentice learns the ways of a warrior. The warrior, as we shall see, seeks the unconscious but does not yield himself to it.

The Impeccable Warrior

After Carlos's encounter with Mescalito and his election as a "chosen one," don Juan begins systematically to teach Carlos how to become accessible to the unconscious. And the more Carlos becomes accessible, the more he needs to know the warrior's path.

The warrior does not regard the unconscious as an enemy, but he knows that if he is lax in his attention, the unconscious may overwhelm him, particularly as he ventures into more alien reaches. The literature of shamanism contains frequent references to the imagery of war. In *Shamanism,* for instance, Mircea Eliade points out that the costumes of Altaic shamans have miniature bows and arrows to frighten the spirits.[95] Dangerous onslaughts of the unconscious are portrayed in dreams by such images as flooding, world war, erupting volcanoes, earthquakes, and powerful animals such as snakes, lions, bears. Dreams also abound with images of being attacked, hunted and imprisoned.

In *Tales of Power* don Juan explains that the upsurge of the unconscious splits one in two. Unless the apprentice has the strength to remain intact and the desire to will himself back to consciousness, it could mean death or a psychosis. (The symptoms he describes actually resemble a schizophrenic state.) All too many people who get involved with the unconscious and with spiritual quests fail to see the dangers in the undertaking. Although there are factors in the unconscious that build up and enrich consciousness, there are also aspects that can tear it down. Negative mother or father complexes, for instance, appear in many guises and hold onto consciousness tenaciously. If we let our guard down at the wrong moment or if we are naive about evil, these complexes can have a very destructive effect and even cause one's death.

As an example, a woman told me recently of a dream in which she was in a car with her mother. Her mother stopped the car near a steep embankment and got out to check something. She "accidentally" left the emergency brake off and the gearshift in neutral. The car began to roll forward, and the dreamer managed to put on the brake just before the car was to go over the edge. On the day following the dream, the woman absentmindedly stepped into the street to cross over when the light turned green. She would have walked right into a car that was speeding through the yellow-to-red light had not another pedestrian grabbed her arm at the last moment. The women was preoccupied with the loss of a relationship at the time, and her dreamy state covered the anger and other very definite affects that were just below the surface. The mother complex was responsible for the blocked emotion and her apparent calm. The dream was a warning of the consequences of being "neutral" about the loss of the relationship and not acknowledging her real feelings.

Even the attempt of the unconscious to heal our psychic wounds can have a destructive effect if the unconscious material is not integrated into everyday life in an authentic way, and if the wisdom of the unconscious is not countered with humor, feeling, everyday tasks and common sense. Von Franz comments on the dangers of an experience of the Self:

> The dark side of the Self is the most dangerous thing of all, precisely because the Self is the greatest power in the psyche. It can cause people to "spin" megalomanic or other delusory fantasies that catch them up and "possess" them. A person in this state thinks with mounting excitement that he has grasped and solved the great cosmic

riddles; he therefore loses all touch with human reality. A reliable symptom of this condition is the loss of one's sense of humor and of human contacts.[96]

I remember a young boy who said he felt like the "world dummy." The unconscious attempted to compensate this one-sided negative image of himself, derived from early childhood experiences, with the equally one-sided image of the savior. He experienced visions and profound insights but had no way of making them personal. He went from one extreme to the other because he could not contain the tension of the opposites. He could not balance the two images and see that he was gifted but no savior, confused but no dummy. While the invasion of the collective unconscious was potentially healing, it was in effect more dangerous than the former negative self-image conditioned by his personal history.

We will now look at some of the different aspects of the path of the warrior. The warrior's attitude is that the worst has already happened; he considers he is already dead and thus has nothing to lose. This same attitude is implicit in the nature of shamanism. Shamans frequently experience their own dismemberment and restoration, and bones or metal replicas of bones are used on their costumes. Mircea Eliade comments:

> By attempting to imitate a skeleton, be it a man's or a bird's, the shamanic costume proclaims the special status of its wearer, who is in some sort one who has been dead and has returned to life. . . .
>
> Shamans are believed to have been killed by the spirits of their ancestors, who, after "cooking" their bodies, counted their bones and replaced them, fastening them together with iron and covering them with new flesh.[97]

The ritual of death and rebirth is an essential aspect of the shaman's experience and the path of knowledge as it occurs all over the world. Because the warrior has experienced the destruction of his old ways and been "cooked" by the unconscious, he can say that he is already dead.

We can consciously encourage and develop in ourselves this attitude of the warrior. For example, there are times when we get cramped with fear and anxiety because, consciously or half consciously, we anticipate the worst. To the extent that we are cramped, our possibilities are limited and determined by our fear; we shrink from the challenge. An alternative in such a situation is, as don Juan recommends, to bring up whatever the worst happens to be and then to accept it. The warrior may deliberately welcome the worst in order to know its secret. The worst may even turn out to be our best chance. If the worst is failure, there may be a tremendous sense of liberation in being able to fail, whether the failure is an examination, a marriage or a job.

In *A Separate Reality,* don Juan explains that the warrior is able to find food because he is not hungry, and is able to stop what it is that hurts him because he is not in pain. Succumbing to hunger and pain is abandon and not the way of a warrior. Hunger and pain are symbolic complexes. They have a strict routine and have the potential to dominate the conscious field. The warrior does not ignore his hunger or his pain—after all, they are part of his path—but he works with these complexes effectively because he does not identify with them or fall into their routines.

The word don Juan uses frequently to describe uncontrolled abandon to a complex is "indulgence." Indulgence is identifying with a complex, whether that complex be the ego or one that arises from the unconscious. If a depressed mood, a power drive or a desire makes its appearance, then to indulge would be to blindly accept the premises, goals and emotions of the complex behind it. As long as we are caught in it, we cannot really see it. Therefore the warrior deliberately gives expression to the mood or desire; he exercises controlled abandon. The warrior's impeccability is his capacity to experience both the unconscious and the ego's frame of reference without identifying with either. Abandon is negative when control is repressed, and control becomes negative when it is split off from its opposite, abandon. Together they form the mood of a warrior, whose way is balance.

Don Juan says that the warrior is a "prisoner of power." By working with the unconscious the warrior encounters his or her fate and personal myth. The warrior is bound, however, to live the task set for him by the unconscious. Although the warrior guards his freedom and avoids the routines of complexes, his only choice with that freedom is to be himself. The warrior seeks to live in relation to his totality, or to what Jung called the archetype of the Self. This totality, however, places demands on the warrior, and thus he is a prisoner of the Self he seeks. As the alchemists have written: "This stone [the philosopher's stone, the goal of the alchemical process] is below thee, as to obedience; above thee, as to dominion."[98] Jung interprets this statement as follows:

> Applied to the self, this would mean: "The self is subordinate to you, yet on the other hand rules you. It is dependent on your own efforts and your knowledge, but transcends you and embraces all those who are of like mind." This refers to the collective nature of the self, since the self epitomizes the wholeness of the personality.[99]

The warrior's way is harmony and balance. The warrior seeks to establish a relationship between the interests of the ego and those of the Self, including all the figures of the unconscious that make claims on him. This way is one of paradox and tension, one in which the opposites are contained. The warrior experiences the ultimate freedom but is a servant, knows the fullness of life but is close to death. The warrior's search for balance shifts the center of the personality from the ego to "a point midway between the conscious and the unconscious."[100] This new center is equivalent to the Chinese concept of the Tao, "the Middle Way and creative centre of all things."[101] (We will return to this concept in the discussion of "the double.")

We have seen the warrior's balance symbolized in the Sioux Indians' use of the pipe. We must also see that it has a dynamic rather than static character. Barbara Meyerhoff discusses this dynamic balance in Huichol culture in *Peyote Hunt*. She raised the question of the differing concepts of balance in Nahua and Western thought with Rafael Gonzalez. He remarked:

> In the West, the "golden mean" is always a condition of compromise reached by reason. *Equilibrio* in the Nahua world seems to be something different, more dynamic. It is a tense balance which comes about not through compromise, but the encounter of two or more unqualified forces meeting headlong and which are not so much reconciled as held teetering on the verge of chaos, not in reason but in experience. In the West the "golden mean" achieves comfort; in the Nahua, *equilibrio* achieves meaning.[102]

The alchemists expressed this dynamic sense of equilibrium with such images as "a warring peace, a sweet wound, a mild evil."[103]

Dreaming and Active Imagination

When Carlos complains about the "vivid dreams and nightmares" he has been having since his experience with Mescalito, don Juan encourages him to learn *dreaming*.[104] *Dreaming* is don Juan's way of dealing with the hyperactivity of the nagual. It is directly analogous to what Jung called active imagination, "the best means ... to reduce an inordinate production of the unconscious"[105]—Carlos's nightmares in this case.

Dreaming, or active imagination, is the activity in which the delicate balance of the warrior's controlled abandon reaches its height. If, because of anxiety, there is too much control, then consciousness is cramped and the unconscious images cannot arise and unfold. If, however, there is too much abandon, then one goes to sleep, or the ego simply goes unconscious, and one does not remember the experience.

In both *dreaming* and active imagination, the conscious personality actively participates in the unfolding of an unconscious process, either by introducing consciousness into an ongoing dream or by bringing up the unconscious while awake. In both methods one is expected to act in a dream or fantasy as one would at any other time. Describing this process, Jung writes:

> You start with any image.... Contemplate it and carefully observe how the picture begins to unfold or to change. Don't try to make it into something, just do nothing but observe what its spontaneous changes are. Any mental picture you contemplate in this way will sooner or later change through a spontaneous association that causes a slight alteration of the picture. You must carefully avoid impatient jumping from one subject to another. Hold fast to the one image you have chosen and wait until it changes by itself. Note all these changes and eventually step into the picture yourself, and if it is a speaking figure at all then say what you have to say to that figure and listen to what he or she has to say.[106]

The pattern of active imagination is the pattern we find in a shaman's journey to the other world, or the hero's journey to the land of the dead in classical literature. There are, for instance, precise parallels to the warrior's practice of *dreaming* in the advice given to Odysseus by Circe as he prepares to travel to the land of the dead to seek the far-seeing counsel of Teiresias, the wise old man:

> Then slash a black ewe's throat, and a black ram,
> facing the gloom of Erebos; but turn
> your head away toward Ocean. You shall see, now,
> souls of the buried dead in shadowy hosts,
> and now you must call out to your companions
> to flay those sheep the bronze knife has cut down,
> for offerings, burnt flesh to those below,
> to sovereign Death and pale Persephone.
> Meanwhile draw sword from him, crouch down, ward off
> the surging phantoms from the bloody pit
> until you know the presence of Teiresias.[107]

In other words, to obtain the insights and foreknowledge of the underworld or unconscious, we have to sacrifice the energy (ewes and rams) that ordinarily flows to the concerns of everyday life. A difficulty then arises: as the process of active imagination comes alive, many things immediately call for our attention, like the phantoms Odysseus must ward off with his sword, his unyielding intent, until Teiresias arrives. This part of the passage reflects Jung's injunction to "hold fast to the one image you have chosen."

Arnold Mindell has illuminated the process of active imagination by drawing parallels between it and the Jewish legend of the creation of the golem. Interpreting the fact that the golem is created on the Sabbath to perform the housework that the rabbi himself cannot do, Mindell writes:

> The ego accomplishes what it can in the course of an average workaday week, so to speak, and then must rest; this is the time for active imagination—when one has lived as far as one can on one's ego resources yet one's "home" is still not in order. Active imagination is not a substitute for active living. It is a point of departure for renewing one's approach to life. To investigate the "holy," the unconscious, to find (or rediscover) the meaning of life is the purpose of the "Sabbath"—on whatever day of the week it occurs. And the active imagination must terminate at the close of this holy day for the ego to resume its daily, active, normal existence.[108]

Mindell observes that the word "TRUTH" needs to be written on the forehead of the golem to affirm the truth and autonomy of the unconscious, but:

> the golem must be reduced back to earth by reversing the letters on its forehead, by tracing the reversed circle of the one outlined at his creation, or by erasing the *e* from *emeth* so that it reads *death* instead of *truth*. Psychologically, these are important steps in concluding active imagination. Experiences must not be forgotten or neglected. When one fails to reflect upon the process which has occurred, one loses the road back into ordinary existence. When fantasies run on and on, spilling autonomously into reality, the golem is still alive. This run-on quality demonstrates a lack of conscious reflection.[109]

Because of the dangers of active imagination, God, in one version of the golem legend, has the rabbi take a partner in his creation:

> Man has unwittingly been fooled by unconscious figures since his beginnings; but if an analyst or friendly helper questions the information presented in active imagination, one is forced to reevaluate and to become conscious of the *relativity* of the wisdom of the unconscious (as the psychotic cannot).[110]

Regarding the use of the unconscious as an aid and not as a substitute, it is preferable in a conflict situation to first make a conscious decision and then to see what the unconscious thinks about it. This approach outwits the timidity and laziness of the ego and also does not impoverish the authority of consciousness. I recall being confronted with a major decision in Zurich. Before making the decision, I wanted to discuss a dream with my analyst since I felt it would shed some light on the issue. He shocked me by asking for my decision before he would discuss the dream. He saw that I was in danger of making my decision only on the basis of the dream interpretation; the decision would have been undermined by my lack of conscious participation. Of course, the reverse would be true for someone who identified with the ego and underestimated the importance of unconscious factors.

The particular procedure or form of active imagination one chooses is an individual matter. The images often demand to be concretized, but some people are not comfortable with, for instance, painting; they may choose to write out their dialogues with the unconscious. Others may prefer dance, clay, sand play, or some other form. The important thing is the active relationship with the unconscious, for that is what secures one on the individual path of knowledge.

The need for active imagination frequently develops in analysis, particularly in a long analysis where it is likely to be suggested and encouraged by dreams. For it to be guided by the analyst, however, is usually inconsistent with the aims of individuation. The role of the guide is dangerous because the guide, as we have seen with don Juan, is easily seduced by his own power drive. There are far too many tales of therapists, shamans, priests and spiritual leaders who succumb to this third enemy of knowledge and presume that they know what is best for the apprentice. Guided fantasy deprives a person of his or her freedom and responsibility. Mindell's advice to have "an analyst or friendly helper" specifically refers to collaboration *after* the event. As Dr. von Franz points out, the use of active imagination is the expression of the integrity of an individual's unique growth process: "No image, no reaction, to the inner images, is prescribed for him; it is the lonely way to one's self, unprotected, but also undisturbed by any guiding hand."[111]

Active imagination or *dreaming* eventually opens the warrior to a related avenue of access to the unconscious, called *seeing*, the next stage in Carlos's development.

4

The Way of the Seer

After Carlos's terrifying bouts with La Catalina, Carlos discontinues the apprenticeship. Two years later, in April 1968, Carlos returns to Mexico with a copy of his first book for don Juan. He has no intention of renewing the apprenticeship, but he quickly realizes how much he has missed the warmth of don Juan's companionship and the depth of his wisdom. Carlos begins once again to make regular trips to see don Juan. He becomes increasingly interested in the phenomenon don Juan calls seeing, *and by November Carlos is ready to try don Juan's smoking mixture again in an effort to* see. *Through his own ability to* see, *don Juan knows that Carlos is capable of* seeing *despite his repeated failures. Don Juan uses the little smoke to overcome Carlos's block and to help him finally to* see.[112]

Forms of Seeing

To *see* is to perceive the unconscious background of any event or situation and thereby to understand things as they are in their totality.

There are three different forms or ways of *seeing* that occur in Carlos's work with don Juan. All are accessible without the aid of hallucinogens. The first form of *seeing* is a spontaneous certainty, a sudden and convincing intuition about the nature of things as they really are. The second form of *seeing* is a perception of a spontaneous image that reveals the unconscious or psychic background; we could call it imagining the soul of things. This form of *seeing* is involved, for instance, when don Juan says that people appear to a seer as egg-shaped clusters of luminous fibers. The final form of *seeing* is perception through physical sensations rather than through visual imagery.

A story from *Tales of Power* provides us with an example of the first form of *seeing*.[113] Don Juan and Carlos are sitting in a park in Mexico City. Don Juan asks Carlos to assess a young man who is wearing green pants and a pink shirt, and who is standing near a church unable to make up his mind whether to go in or not. When Carlos is able to halt his internal dialogue, he involuntarily says that the man has a drinking problem. Don Juan confirms his assessment. Don Juan goes on to explain that *seeing* occurs when one spontaneously arrives at a conclusion about another person, a conclusion expressed with great conviction but arrived at without any effort or

71

logical deduction. This form of *seeing* could be called acute intuition, and it is probably the most accessible form. According to the image, we can tap our ability to *see* by posing the question relevant to us in a given situation, by stopping the internal dialogue and by remaining open to what the unconscious produces.

The potential avenues for exploring *seeing* in this way are inexhaustible, but like anything else on the path of knowledge our *seeing* too needs to be tested. One way in particular lends itself easily to this. When confronted by a dream that interests yet puzzles, go into a state of deep relaxation with the dream present in the mind's eye. Frequently, there will spontaneously emerge a clear thought that precisely expresses the point the dream is trying to make, and gives one an idea how to integrate the dream. The advantage of approaching *seeing* in this way is that it keeps us in touch with our own unconscious material; it is also a safeguard against the kind of inflation that may arise when we "read" other people and think we know more about them than they do about themselves.

In the procedure I have outlined, there are four ways we can test and assess the accuracy of our perception. The first indication of proper *seeing* is that the thought or image should strike us as unexpected; it should reveal something we would not have thought consciously. Secondly, we could expect to have the "aha!" experience, a certain "click." Thirdly, as we begin to integrate the dream information, we should find that we have a deeper sense that we are on the right path and that life is flowing once more. Finally, to be sure we are on the right path, and that our *seeing* has not been too influenced by our habitual modes of perception and feeling or by unconscious complexes, we can examine the dreams that follow for corrections to or modifications of our understanding.

Naturally, we can also explore this form of *seeing* in situations where we are in doubt or have a special question that cannot be answered by rational means. At other times, we will find we *see* without any conscious preparation. In these instances it is valuable to observe what the unconscious has produced, rather than to disregard or discount it just because it seems irrational. We all have either experienced this phenomenon or heard others say, "I *knew* that was going to happen, but I just didn't trust my intuition." When we experience such unexpected certainties or images of unfolding events, it would be wise to inspect the information, wait for further confirmation, investigate the information psychologically or take a risk and act on the basis of the information, expectantly testing the validity of the vision.

In the second mode of *seeing*, the unconscious throws up visual images or scenes that may have great significance. (I say "may have," because frequently intuitives or psychics *see* facts about a person's life that are accurate but in no way relevant to the person's life situation; here I am only interested in images that are meaningful.)

An example of this appears in *A Separate Reality,* when don Juan *sees* something crucial about Carlos's past.[114] Don Juan knows Carlos can *see,* but although Carlos follows all the appropriate steps, at the last moment he still fails to *see.* Don Juan is perplexed. Carlos becomes very sad about his failure and unexpectedly begins to talk about his childhood. Don Juan stares at him. Carlos begins to experience a strange warmth centered in his abdominal region, and then don Juan says, "Perhaps it's the promise." Don Juan has just *seen* a promise Carlos made as a child, and he begins to question Carlos about it. Carlos cannot relate in any meaningful way to don Juan's questions, but don Juan persists, saying he *sees* a small boy crying, a frightened little boy who is crying *now.* Suddenly Carlos is flooded with images from his own past, and he recognizes the small boy. The boy is still crying because Carlos had made a promise to him, and the promise is still active. That promise was now holding Carlos back.

What Carlos remembered was a period in his life when he was frequently overwhelmed by the cruelty of his innumerable cousins. He applied himself and learned how to fight and subdue his enemies and rivals. But he did not know how to stop. Then a younger boy at school took a liking to him. Carlos used to tease him, but the boy, Joaquin, still looked up to Carlos and followed him about. One day Carlos was playing a prank and pushed over the blackboard in the classroom. It unexpectedly fell on Joaquin and broke his collarbone. The pain of this experience broke something in Carlos also, and in that moment he promised he would never again try to be victorious if the little Joaquin were healed. The boy recovered, and don Juan was able to *see* that the promise was preventing Carlos from claiming knowledge.

Don Juan was able to tap Carlos's emotion, his abdominal region, and to *see* the place and the moment where Carlos was blocked. Initially don Juan's vision seemed to have little bearing on Carlos's failures to *see* the guardian of the other world. Yet with courage and conviction, don Juan trusted the image and continued to push.

I am reminded of a visit I made with a friend to a psychic in 1970. After my friend had spent her time with the psychic, I went in. The psychic told me she was angry because my friend had not been honest with her. I asked my friend about this later, and she said the psychic had told her that both her children were in good health—she could *see* both of them. My friend protested that she had only one child. The psychic then told her there were certainly two children, and if she did not intend to be honest it would be better for her to leave. As my friend was telling me this, she suddenly remembered that ten years ago she had become pregnant, borne the child and given it up for adoption. Unlike don Juan, the psychic did not pursue the possible meaning of the image she *saw*.

In the story of Carlos's promise, we see a primary condition for *seeing*, namely an emotional urgency—something is wrong! We turn to the unconscious when we have exhausted the conscious means available to us and still remain stuck. A second important feature in that account is that when don Juan stared at Carlos his eyes became foggy, went out of focus. To *see*, that is, we have to allow our vision of the moment to blur somewhat; otherwise we are held to the present and to our conscious perceptions. The lack of conscious focus creates a "hole," an opening for the unconscious image.

Another important element in that story is that don Juan had once made such a promise himself. Don Juan tells Carlos that during the great Yaqui wars at the end of the nineteenth century, his mother and father were killed by the Mexicans. Don Juan himself was beaten and had his hands broken by the soldiers. His father was not killed immediately but died from the wounds while he was being transported with his seven-year-old son, prisoners in a box car. Before his father died, don Juan promised him that he would one day kill his parents' assassins. Over the years, however, the promise was dropped because don Juan saw that the oppressed and the oppressors are one; they are unconsciously identified with each other. He learned to escape the division of these opposites so that he was no longer held by his hate or his promise. What this illustrates is that we are better able to *see* something about another person if we have had a similar experience ourselves.

For an example of the third mode of *seeing*, through physical sensations, consider Carlos's visit to Sacateca, a man of knowledge.[115] When Carlos went to Sacateca in 1962, Sacateca immediately sensed something wrong. He danced to *see* what it was. His dance involved partially closing his eyes, tapping the floor with his right foot placed behind the heel of his left foot and slowly lifting his right arm with his palm open, perpendicular to the ground, fingers pointing toward Carlos. At this point Carlos became restless and apprehensive. Surprised by his own reaction and completely dissassociated, Carlos turned abruptly and left without a word. Sacateca's intuition was verified: Carlos had come to pick his brains, not for friendship.

Sacateca, like don Juan, allowed his eyes to go out of focus. Then he used the rhythmic activity of foot-tapping to lower the level of his consciousness. In that way he could apprehend the unconscious picture of what was happening. Rhythmic activity, indeed, is common throughout the world as a means of achieving a trance state in order to have a visionary experience. Finally, however, it was through the movement of his hand that Sacateca was able to *see*. The knowledge was unconsciously picked up by Carlos, who fled in consternation.

The means of *seeing* through the experience of the body is not uncommon. Hand trembling is used throughout the Americas as a means of divination. The shaman allows his hand to pass over the body of the person who is ill; when his hand begins to tremble, he knows the location and nature of the illness. And there is the account of the Todos Santos shaman who is asked by a farmer to tell him who has stolen his hen, and whether or not it is still alive.[116] The shaman rolls up the right leg of his trousers, puts his left hand on the calf of his leg below the knee, closes his eyes, mumbles softly, and after about three minutes comes up with the information the farmer wanted. The shaman explained that the muscles of his leg had spoken to him. The Charismatic Movement offers another example with its use of "the laying on of hands," although here, as with any "technique," one must be very cautious about the motivation and character of the practitioner.

We may experience this particular way of *seeing,* though perhaps in a modified form, by paying close attention to our physical reactions in the presence of another person. If an emotion is constellated in the other person, and their awareness of it is being repressed, then we may very well pick up physical symptoms related to that emotion. I recall the beginning of an hour with an analysand, for instance, when I began to feel nauseous. I could find no basis in myself for the physical symptom, and so I asked the woman if there was something going on she was not telling me. Something "clicked," and she poured out a very emotional story involving her "sick" feelings about a particular relationship. As soon as she began to talk, my nausea went away. I had *seen* something, though I didn't know what it was.

Emotions are contagious. Our bodies react to them and provide us with key information about what is going on, in our own unconscious or in the unconscious of someone we are close to. At times, it seems that an emotion so constellated *wants* to surface and *will* surface through the person who is more conscious or who has least resistance to it.[117]

In a similar way, there are times when we experience a sexual

feeling for someone when we really have no sexual inclination toward that person. The sudden, irrational feeling of desire may point
to the fact that something is missing in the conscious relationship,
that there is some other feeling, in one or both parties, that is not
being expressed. Instinct then compensates the lack of feeling in the
conscious relationship. If we do not know this fundamental, psychological reality, we are likely to focus on the sexuality and miss the
real feeling. (The feelings that come up through the body as sexual,
incidentally, may not always be positive. We can just as well be
unconsciously angry at a person and then experience the physical
attraction, or we may experience desire because the other person is
unaware of their anger.)

What is common to all three modes of *seeing* is a lowering of
consciousness. The warrior, in fact, deliberately tries to lower his
consciousness in order to grasp what is happening beyond the edge
of his awareness. The lowering of consciousness, of course, involves
a loss of energy, and the question always arises of how to reclaim
this energy. Von Franz, for instance, tells the story of a palm reader
who could pick up an immense amount of information about someone as soon as they entered the room, but he needed to focus on the
person's palm, and thereby lower his consciousness, in order to tap
his intuitions.[118] The man then had to literally "paw" his clients
before they left in order to get his energy back and not be left
feeling empty. This habit naturally created misunderstandings and ill
feeling in many of his clients. Von Franz goes on to stress the
importance for the therapist or analyst of regaining energy, "refilling
the gas tank," without damaging his or her family, analysands or
others. The therapist needs time alone for creative work, active
imagination or some other activity that generates energy and restores
what is lost.

Having examined *seeing* from these different perspectives, we will
now talk about what Carlos actually *sees* and about the effects of
seeing upon the consciousness of the one who *sees*.

The Guardian

At the beginning of the process of learning to *see*, don Juan has
Carlos attempt to *see* the guardian of the other world. Carlos uses
don Juan's pipe to "smoke" the guardian. He loses bodily control
and tumbles over on his side. Don Juan then orders him to stare
with his left eye at a place on the ground directly in front of him.
The first thing Carlos sees is a gnat. Next, he becomes aware that he
is standing up and looking straight ahead. It is then that he sees an

enormous horrifying animal, perhaps one hundred feet tall. This strange animal is the guardian. The image of the guardian becomes clear to Carlos gradually as he puts it together piece by piece. It has two buggy eyes, two short wings enabling it to skid lightly above the ground with incredible speed. When Carlos encounters the guardian a second time about two months later, other features begin to stand out—its large, drooling mouth, its slick, shiny scales, ugly tufts of hair, and the fact that each part of the guardian seems to be alive as though the guardian had a million eyes.[119]

Before we examine why the guardian takes this specific form in relation to Carlos, we will look into the phenomenon of the guardian itself. The symbol of the guardian is not unique to don Juan's world but is characteristic of religions and mythologies all over the world. Among the ancient Greeks, for instance, there was Cerberus at the gates of Hades, and among Christians there is the archangel Michael at the gates of Paradise. A guardian figure always stands between this world and the other world, whether paradise or the land of the dead.

In *Tales of Power* don Juan tells Carlos that in the development of consciousness, we inevitably build up a form of protection against the overwhelming influence of the unconscious, and that this protection serves the necessary and purposive function of allowing the ego to develop its strength. He explains, however, that the guardian of consciousness gradually claims so much power that it becomes a prison guard, with us as the prisoner. The guardian, in other words, is the symbolic expression of those aspects of the personality that once protected Carlos from his unconscious but that now prevent him from re-establishing the broken connection. The guardian expresses the basic defense structure inherent in every personality. This natural phenomenon can be distinguished from the defense mechanisms of the neurotic. The guardian is closer to what in psychiatry is called "character defenses," integral aspects of the personality such as the tendency to strive for power, prestige or perfection, or such as being excessively kind or excessively fanciful. The guardian is the symbolic expression of the routines of our conscious adaptation to life. These routines at one time provided structure and support but they eventually stand in the way of purposive attempts to get in touch with the unconscious. The guardian is the sum of our own most obstinate tendencies.

In trying to understand what the guardian is for Carlos, we need to see what this strange creature reveals about Carlos's personality. Mindell in his work on Castaneda's material pointed out that the gaping, drooling mouth of the guardian referred to Carlos's tendency to talk instead of act. Carlos routinely talks in an excessive way and uses his mouth to avoid contact with himself, don Juan or the unconscious. As a verification of this understanding of the guardian, Mindell noted that Carlos immediately begins to talk after his experience with the guardian, and don Juan complains about him being a "blabbermouth."

Carlos has another characteristic that also bars him from the unconscious: his tendency to be suspicious—to suspect that someone is tricking him and to seek reasonable explanations for everything. This suspiciousness, which prevents him from seeing or accepting the meaningfulness of his experiences with the unconscious, is symbolized by the guardian's million eyes. We find a parallel in Greek mythology in the figure of Argos, who has a thousand eyes and guards Zeus's mistress from the jealous eyes of Hera, his wife. The eyes symbolize anxious watchfulness. The guardian's tendency to skid above the ground is also symbolic, expressing Carlos's skittishness and his habit of not quite being down to earth.

Finally, there is the peculiar identity between the monstrous guardian and the gnat. Don Juan says that the guardian to the other world is a gnat. This implies that all of the things that characterize us and block us from the unconscious seem small and insignificant when they first appear to consciousness. The habits of consciousness, however, are so engrained and deep-seated that they are also enormous, frightening and almost impossible to overcome, ignore or step around.

Don Juan says that before one can cross over into the unconscious, the guardian must become nothing: only true *seeing* allows the guardian to become nothing. In *The Second Ring of Power*, La Gorda refers to this process as "losing the human form."[120] *Seeing* is more than the ability to perceive images; it is the deep and transforming insight into the nature of things. Deep insight transforms and overcomes the guardian; this is not accomplished with the ego.

We can begin to get a sense of our own guardian by observing closely our routines (extraversion, introversion, motherliness, fatherliness, intellectualization, and so on). Considering the guardian as a personification of our resistance to the unconscious, we can also play with the image more loosely and find the guardian turning up in unexpected ways. For instance, I was once going up a ski lift for the first run with a friend from Zurich, and as we were talking on the lift, I brought up the issue of the guardian. I was playing with ideas about what the guardian was when my friend noted that a moment before I had complained of a little knee pain, saying I had better be cautious. He looked at me and intuitively remarked that right at the moment, it seemed that the guardian for me was my knee pain. In other words, the thing that stood between me and an experience of exhilaration on the slopes was the caution symbolized by my knee pain. I took his remark to heart and was pleased to find that I had no further pain or difficulty on the slopes.

To summarize then, we can isolate the various aspects of the guardian by becoming more aware of those moments when we are guarded.

The Luminous Egg and the Will

When you learn to *see,* don Juan says, you will see that all people are luminous eggs, composed of fine threads of light circulating from the head to the navel. And you will see that people are in touch with the world around them through long fibers of light that extend from the center of the abdomen. These fibers are responsible for the warrior's unique balance and stability. Don Juan calls these particular fibers the will.

Seeing reveals the essence of what is. Therefore, if we investigate the symbol of the luminous egg as don Juan describes it, we will have some indication of how he understands the essential nature of being human. First of all, the egg symbolizes wholeness and potential; or, turning it slightly, the egg is our own potential wholeness. The symbol of the luminous egg resonates with other religious traditions such as Taoism and Western alchemy. In the alchemical tradition the spherical light, the fire inside of God, is narrowed to a point. It is also the shining and illuminating body that dwells in the heart of man.[121] In alchemy also, the arcane substance is likened to an egg.[122] The arcane substance is that which contains the opposites in their uncombined form as the beginning of all things.[123] The egg condition is the precondition of the philosopher's stone, the symbol of the goal of the process of individuation. The light or luminosity of the egg is related to what the alchemists saw as the divine spark that appears in nature, including human nature.

The luminous egg appears in Taoist thought as the golden flower: "The Golden Flower is the Light . . . the true power of the transcendent Great *One*."[124] The Taoists also speak of the light going in a circle. For them, the circulation of the light, like the circulation of don Juan's luminous fibers, is what they call the "backward flowing method." This circulation is the introversion of one's libido or attention, and the circulation of that attention is the process of self-reflection. Out of this inward vision, there comes not only a knowledge of ourselves from the heights to the depths but also the crystalization of that which is divine in us. The circulation of the light in time creates the center of the personality. It is for this reason that the Taoists say the circulation of the light creates the natural spirit-body, the essential consciousness of the individual that transcends time and space and will continue after death. The spirit-body is the awareness of one's luminosity; it is the double.

Don Juan's understanding of the will is a natural extension of his vision of man as a luminous egg. The will is composed of tentacle-like fibers emerging from a person's body in the area of the solar plexus. The emergence of the will is the natural result of the circulation of the light, or of the process of the gradual illumination in our awareness of our totality. These luminous fibers, don Juan says, join a person to the outer world. The will is a relation between the center of the personality and the ongoing life in which the warrior partici-pates. We are told later that the will directs the warrior's acts, that it defies common sense, and that the warrior becomes conscious of the emerging will as he performs impossible acts and as impossible things keep happening to him. The will is that force which saves a warrior when apparently there is no escape from doom. It is the unaccountable factor that decides an issue in favor of life. The will is symbolic, therefore, of the deepest instinctive core of the personality and its attachment to life. The will is the relation between three-dimensional reality and the larger personality that is trying to actual-ize itself in life.

I think this description of the will conforms to the evidence. For instance, when don Juan says that the warrior's will enables him to perform impossible acts and experience impossible things, he is say-ing that there is an equation between the appearance of the will and synchronistic phenomena. Synchronistic events are more likely to occur when one has a living relationship to the Self. Synchronistic events are those meaningful coincidences that impress us with the oneness of inner and outer experience. For instance, when we experience an inner sense of harmony we find that outer conflicts are resolved without any conscious effort, or we dream of a particu-lar creative project and a friend drops by the next day with a book precisely about the subject of our interest.[125]

Jung often talked of psychic life in terms of the image of the spectrum. The infra-red end of the spectrum is the realm of the instincts, whereas at the ultra-violet end we find the archetypes, symbolic representations of the same processes that appear in the instinctive realm. We apprehend the archetypes through the psychic sphere and the instincts through the physical sphere. Both are mani-festations of the same phenomenon, just as the two ends of the spectrum are but different aspects of the phenomenon of light. At the physical end of the spectrum, we find the will as an instinctive force, and at the psychological end we find the archetype of the Self. The will provides the necessary balance to the effects of *seeing*. *Seeing*, don Juan tells us, detaches us from the world, exposes its folly. Will, on the other hand, reunites us with the world and with the principle of life. As an expression of relation to the world, it is the drive of the transpersonal within us to become conscious, or to become actualized in the world through us. Our own totality seeks to come into being with the will as its expression. In this sense we can either thwart the designs of the will or, as don Juan says, temper it until it is neat and wholesome and utterly reliable.

Don Juan later tells Carlos that one first becomes aware of the will as a warm spot that cannot be soothed, and that this warm spot eventually becomes an intense pain and finally convulsions. He says that the power of the will is as strong as one's suffering. This statement about the will is reminiscent of Jung's comment that the strength of the drive toward individuation (the will) is only as strong as the symptoms. The will is the Tao, the functioning of nature at its deepest level. Like the will the Tao makes things happen and creates balance. It is said of the Tao; "The high it presses down, the low it lifts up. The excessive it takes from, the deficient it gives to."[126]

We will turn now to the seer's controlled folly, the attitude that emerges from the tendency of the seer's vision to separate him from life and the tendency of his will to keep him attached to life.

Controlled Folly

For don Juan one of the results of *seeing* is the recognition that our own acts and the acts of our fellows are folly. A warrior controls his folly by acting as though things mattered in the face of knowledge that nothing matters. Don Juan explains that it is his will that "controls the folly" of his life and makes him go on living. It does not matter to him that nothing matters.[127]

A warrior exercises his controlled folly in all of his interactions with the world except when dealing with the allies of knowledge. One never *sees* the ally itself but only the form the ally takes at the moment, whereas the warrior can *see* his or her fellow creatures. The impersonal force of the archetype or ally assumes various forms or symbolic representations, and yet we can never see the archetype in itself. We are always dealing with images or representations—"the hero with a thousand faces," for instance. We can see the folly of the thousand and one things that entrap our attention, but the ally is a suprapersonal force whose origin is a mystery beyond our grasp.

It will help to understand controlled folly if we separate control and folly. The folly of life is characterized by the collective and personal routines of consciousness. Our folly is our identity with everyday life where we look but never *see* beyond our attachments and involvements. The refusal to identify with everyday life—what Jung called the provisional attitude—is equally unconscious, equally folly. With the provisional attitude one feels that the present is not quite "the real thing." Real life is always somewhere in the future, and if the present is by any chance disagreeable, one is under no obligation to live it. A person with the provisional attitude senses the folly that the warrior *sees,* but his will is not sufficiently developed to help him experience fully and assume responsibility for his folly. The warrior's will controls his folly because it organizes his folly in a meaningful pattern. The warrior is in control of his folly because he sees the larger symbolic process that is trying to become conscious through him and his life situation.

It is through self-awareness and through the understanding of the meaning of our experience that we control our folly. In 1932, Jung lectured on the psychological foundation of kundalini yoga and discussed a concept that parallels don Juan's controlled folly. In the tradition of kundalini yoga a distinction is made between two different aspects of the experience of the various chakras, the *sthula* and the *suksma* aspects: "The *sthula* aspect is simply things as we see them. The *suksma* aspect is what we guess about them, or the abstractions or philosophical conclusions which we draw from observed facts."[128]

Jung gave an example of these two aspects as they would appear in a relationship between two people. When we love someone, we are identified with the other person and together we live unconsciously in a *participation mystique*. We therefore repress our own individuality and the individuality of our partner. As a result, resistances begin to develop and we experience bad moods, disappointments and attacks of hatred or fear. Through these negative emotions in the *sthula* aspect, we are separated from the person we love. If we view this from the *suksma* aspect, we see that the unconscious is separating us in order for each of us to realize our differences and our individuality. As Jung said, "We learn that what is a regrettable habit perhaps, or impossible moods, or inexplicable disagreements in the *sthula* aspect, is something quite different in the *suksma* aspect."[129] The meaning of the *suksma* aspect controls the folly of the *sthula* aspect. "If a person thoroughly understands this ... he knows when he loves that soon he will hate. Therefore he will laugh when he is going uphill and weep when he is going downhill, like Till Eulenspiegel."[130]

Control and folly belong together. Control without folly isolates us from life and prevents us from realizing anything; folly without control submerges us in unconsciousness and prevents the growth of our individuality. We found this same kind of union earlier in the combination of the devil's weed and the little smoke. The devil's weed immerses us in the folly of passion, ambition and power, and yet it leads to the little smoke, the objectivity that allows us to *see* the deeper meaning of the symbolic life that is trying to realize itself through our folly.

5

Shamanic Flight

Carlos and don Juan are sitting at a table in a restaurant in Mexico City. Don Juan is not wearing the familiar khakis and sandals, but rather a custom-tailored suit, because today he intends to teach Carlos about the tonal and the nagual and about the "totality of oneself." He explains that everyone has two different sides, a pair of opposites, one the tonal and the other the nagual. The tonal, he says as he touches his chest, is this person, everything we know and everything for which we have a word. The nagual, on the other hand, is everything that is unknown. At birth we are all nagual, but gradually the tonal begins to emerge and to groom itself until a time comes when only the tonal is recognized.

To illustrate this, don Juan refers to the restaurant table and to all of the items on the table as an island surrounded by a vast sea. The table is the island of the tonal. Everything that we know exists on the island, and everything that is unknown and cannot be spoken of surrounds the island. Men and women of knowledge not only know and observe the effects of the nagual upon the island, but they also transport themselves into the nagual's time.[131]

The Tonal and the Nagual

Carlos's meeting with don Juan in Mexico City, and don Juan's presence in a custom-tailored suit, represent a breakthrough in terms of Carlos's development. Most people, as don Juan says, do not recognize the nagual and cannot see beyond the world of appearances, the tonal. In following Carlos to this point, however, we have seen and heard very little of his relationship to the everyday world and have been acquainted primarily with his adventures with the nagual. Don Juan's suit and the meeting in Mexico City, therefore, call specific attention to the fact that everything don Juan stands for is meant to be integrated in the everyday world of business, traffic, money, apartment living, taxes, relationships and so on. Carlos's shock of disbelief when he sees don Juan in a suit indicates his failure to acknowledge the need to transform his daily life through the knowledge he has gained from his experiences of the nagual.

As the island of consciousness, the tonal is the sum of our various descriptions of ourselves and the world. It is, more accurately, the innate tendency that creates order out of chaos, that structures and

84

organizes our experience and that brings into being our character, life situation and worldview.

Don Juan says there is a personal and a collective tonal. The personal tonal is our distinct personality and particular perception of the world. Because we all live in a collective environment (America, Los Angeles, Mexico, Mexico City, etc.), we also partake of a collective description of the world that we share with others or disagree about with others. Whether we agree or disagree about our description, whether we are Republicans or Democrats, we are engulfed by the collective tonal. As examples of contrasting collective tonals, the Indian tonal says that the earth is our mother who must be honored, thanked and protected, whereas the American tonal says, at least until recently, that the earth is an object to be used to our most immediate advantage. The Indian tonal says that spirits are external to us and may have abodes in particular places in the landscape, whereas the Western tonal says that spirits are psychological complexes that have been projected onto objects, places and persons in the environment. In elaborating on the personal and collective tonal, don Juan mentions that the Indians have lost both their personal tonal and the collective tonal.[132] Individually and collectively, Native Americans have been oppressed and discriminated against and have had their worldview overwhelmed, challenged and discredited by the technological consciousness and peculiar brand of rationality that belongs to Western culture.

We can see the same destruction of the tonal in other cultures. Jung tells, for instance, of the loss of the tonal he witnessed among the Elgonyi tribe in Africa.[133] In 1925, while staying with the Elgonyi, Jung asked an old medicine man about dreams. The man's eyes filled with tears, and he said, "In old days the *laibons* [medicine men] had dreams, and knew whether there is war or sickness or whether rain comes and where the herds should be driven."[134] He informed Jung that since the white men arrived no one had dreams anymore, or at least not big dreams. "Dreams were no longer needed because now the English knew everything!"[135] The medicine man was the "living embodiment" of the destruction of the African tonal or, as Jung says, "of the spreading disintegration of an undermined, out-moded, unrestorable world."[136]

Don Juan's description of the tonal existing in the sea of the nagual parallels the imagery we find in dreams and, frequently, in creation myths and fairytales. Myths from the most divergent cultures describe the original creation as an act of bringing mud up from the bottom of the sea to make land in the midst of the primeval waters, the matrix of everything unknown and unknowable. In dreams we frequently see the ego and the durability of one's conscious world threatened by tidal waves and floods. Often conscious life is shown in dreams as having become mechanical, boring, lifeless and dry; the dreamer may then be led to a spring, a well, a flowing river or to the ocean where the living waters of the nagual can quench the individual's thirst for renewal.

Much of Carlos's work in his apprenticeship thus far has been designed to fulfill the task of what don Juan calls cleaning the island of the tonal. Cleaning the island of the tonal refers to physical health, emotional stability, a good adaptation to one's social and economic context and to developing a consciousness that can withstand stress and conflict. Cleaning the mess on one's island is one of the major tasks of the impeccable hunter or warrior. Although the cleaning work may involve establishing one's position in outer life, the more essential aspect of a proper tonal is the realization of a strong, vigorous and balanced conscious attitude. It is more accurate and valuable to emphasize the quality of one's individual conscious attitude than the more variable items of one's island such as profession, salary, marital status, etc.

Don Juan says that the nagual is used to prop up the tonal. Struggling with the unconscious, as in the analytic process, is something that strengthens the ego. The Jungian way of formulating this is to say that the integration of the shadow does more than anything else to give solidity and strength to the ego. In other words, when the shadowy things that we traditionally like to deny, like sexuality, greed, aggression, anger, laziness and so on, exist close to the shore of our island, we will be far more secure in our comings and goings if we are familiar with these shoals and reefs. We are weakened and undermined by our unconsciousness of the shadow because our shadowy tendencies exert their influence on us all the more treacherously when we ignore them. Most of what we refer to as therapy consists of the process of integrating the shadow, using the unconscious to prop up the ego and cleaning the island.

Don Juan goes on to introduce the concept of a proper tonal, one characterized by balance and equilibrium. He says that each tonal has two sides, an active, rugged side and a softer side connected more with decision and judgment. Although don Juan does not refine these distinctions, I think he has in mind something like Jung's concept of two conscious attitudes, introversion and extraversion. Introversion is the tendency for our attention and psychic energy to flow inward and to be focused on subjective experience, whereas extraversion is the tendency for psychic energy to flow toward an outer object. The balance of the proper tonal would suggest that the individual has developed both aspects of the personality so that he or she is not limited to the one attitude that is more natural and comfortable.

Typically for don Juan, when he introduces the concept of the proper tonal he encourages Carlos to translate it into experience. He first of all has Carlos assess the tonal of the people passing by. As Carlos examines the people and comments on his perception of the strength or weakness of their tonal, he is led to recognize the various forms of indulgence, the ways in which people make their tonal weak by cultivating their timidity, their boredom, their submissiveness, etc. We groom our weaknesses just as diligently as Chinese women of the upper class worked at retarding the growth of their feet.

Don Juan has Carlos wait for a proper tonal to appear. A woman passes by who is attractive and well-dressed and who gives Carlos the immediate impression of being in harmony with herself and her surroundings. Don Juan confirms Carlos's assessment—she has the quality of a potential warrior. Don Juan insists that Carlos at least speak with the woman. He is forced to make the experience of a proper tonal real and complete.

When I was thinking of this particular passage some time ago, I decided to observe people in terms of their tonal and to see if I would come across someone with a proper tonal during the day. I was at the bank when the idea struck me, and from there I went to the post office. When I got out of the car to drop letters in the mailbox, I saw a woman in her mid-thirties whom I had met in Mexico six months ago. After a moment of recognition and a brief conversation, I realized that here was the proper tonal I had been looking for. Curiously enough, even though we live in the same small town, I had not seen her once since our meeting in Mexico, nor have I seen her again since. What stood out about her was that she had a solid marriage, a strong commitment to her family and a keen sense of her own individuality. She had a good adaptation to the outer world and also shared with her husband a Christian faith that was based on deep inner experience. The religious life for her was a response to an inner demand and not an adaptation to tradition.

Returning to the nagual, we see that even though it is unknowable and unfathomable, it does produce effects on conscious life. Following the image of the sea and the island, the nagual produces effects on the shorelines or borders of consciousness. It creates subtle as well as drastic changes in the shape of our world. It produces strange creatures that are alien to us, that belong to another environment quite unlike our own. It tosses onto the shore wreckage, things that have slipped into the sea and the garbage we have deposited there. Things which once belonged to consciousness have either slipped back into the unconscious, out of sight, or have been repressed or forgotten. The unconscious then quite spontaneously reproduces these things, though somewhat altered by the water. In a more interior way, when we meditate with the sea, that interaction also produces something in us—inspirations, insights, moods, creative ideas and thoroughly unexpected fantasies. From the effects of the nagual, we deduce that it is the source of spontaneous creativity and of meaningful inner and outer experiences, whether the experiences be dreams, fantasies, intuitions or symbolic events in outer life.

Don Juan teaches Carlos to notice the momentary effects of the nagual. Carlos has just experienced a shiver, and don Juan encourages him to pay attention to what was going on when the shiver passed through his body, because at that moment the nagual surfaced. As a parallel story I remember an evening with friends in Zurich when *Tales of Power* had just been published. One of our group was trying to say something about the nagual. "The nagual," he began, "is, uh . . . ," and then he went blank. His mouth was open but nothing would come out. Immediately, another person spoke up and said, "That's right! That's the nagual!" The nagual had indeed produced its effect. When the nagual surfaces in the body, as a loss of speech, a twitch, a groan or a yawn, then the ego has the opportunity to become aware that there is something else at work, something opposed to our conscious attention or at least different from it, something that defies our attempts at regulation. The effects of the nagual offer us a momentary glimpse of our totality. Just as we are capable of driving without being conscious of the fact that we are driving, so we can also experience the effects of the nagual on the body without noticing the existence or the meaningfulness of this other dimension.

Don Juan explains that our eyes belong to the tonal, and that we must learn to blink when we experience the nagual. Our eyes are adjusted to the ego's description of the world; they have been trained by exposure to the tonal. Our vision tends to be overwhelmed by the images and experiences produced by the nagual for they do not fit the description of the reality we are accustomed to. The ability to blink the eyes is the ability to break the spell of the unconscious. It is the ability to carry with us into the other world the thread of who we are in everyday life. Blinking is the shield composed of the items that have heart for the warrior. (It is interesting to note that schizophrenics do not blink with as high a frequency as others; they are inundated by the unconscious.)

As a warrior progresses along the path of knowledge, he sets up a "customs house" between the tonal and the nagual. The customs house, don Juan says, is his intent. The warrior at this stage has progressed far enough to be able to detach a portion of his consciousness from the tonal; that is, he has developed an observing ego. With the observing ego the warrior is able to discriminate between the tonal and the nagual and to know which world he is dealing with. He is able to choose in any given situation whether he wants to relate to the tonal or the nagual. The warrior can focus on the unconscious background (the *suksma* aspect referred to earlier) through reflection or active imagination, or he can choose to focus on and interact with things as they are (the *sthula* aspect). Don Juan's image of the customs house expresses the fact that the warrior's observing ego has become a psychic mid-point identified with neither the tonal nor the nagual.

A customs house or observing ego enables us, for instance, when we experience an emotion such as rage or fear, to choose whether we want to act out the emotion or to pursue its deeper meaning. It is also helpful in discriminating between the conscious and unconscious content in our interactions with others. A young woman, for example, tells her mother she has developed an interest in painting and shows her her most recent piece. The mother responds with enthusiasm and then recommends that her daughter take a class from one of the well-known art instructors at the university. The mother thinks she is being supportive and empathetic with her daughter. The daughter, however, hears that whatever she does is never going to be good enough just as it is. She responds to her mother with hurt or anger; the mother is perplexed, and the daughter is left feeling both guilty and misunderstood. But what is the truth? Was the daughter experiencing an unconscious content in her mother, or her own negative mother complex? As the young woman learns to differentiate between the visible or audible surface of her relationship with her mother and the constellation of the negative mother complex, she will know whether she is dealing with the tonal or the nagual and be able to behave accordingly.

When don Juan mentioned the tonal and nagual to Carlos for the first time, Carlos referred to his own knowledge of these two concepts from anthropological literature. He assumes that the tonal is a guardian spirit, usually an animal associated with the day of one's birth, and that the nagual is the name given to either a man or woman of knowledge or to a person capable of transformation into an animal. Don Juan corrects Carlos's understanding of the tonal: he says it is not an animal guardian but rather a guardian that can be symbolized by a particular animal.

While in Zurich I discovered a monograph, *Nagualism*, written by Daniel Brinton in 1894, that amplifies the two terms tonal and nagual. The word *tonalli* is translated from the Nahuatl language to mean the unique individuality of a person. Brinton confirms that the tonal is the preconscious individuality with which a person is born, and which can either be strengthened or weakened throughout life. The astrological natal chart is an attempt to articulate the same information as the *tonalli*, and in fact, just as the astrological sun sign says a great deal about the conscious attitude, so the word *tonalli* is derived from the radical *tona*, meaning to warm or be warm, and is related to *tonatiuh*, the sun.[137]

In the eighteenth century, when much of this information on nagualism was collected, the belief was held (and still is today among many people) that the guardian spirit or tonal could wander and become lost or stolen, causing sickness or misfortune for the individual. We have the same "loss of soul" experience when we are overtaken by apathy, depression, sickness and other disorders. The Indians would call in a shaman for such a person, and the shaman would perform a ceremony called "the restitution of the tonal."[138] The purpose of the ceremony was to retrieve the guardian spirit and bring the patient back into a right relationship with himself and his natural vitality and enthusiasm. A therapist is often like the *tetonaltiani*, "he who concerns himself with the tonal."[139] Brinton also confirms the idea that the man of knowledge is the one who builds a bridge to the nagual. He points out that in the Nahuatl language the root *na* contains the idea of "to know" or "knowledge."[140] The first missionary accounts from Spain speak of the *naualli*, "masters of mystic knowledge."

The Spanish Catholics were disturbed by the nagualists' adoration of their naguals, their allies. Brinton cites the Bishop of Chiapas in 1692 commanding that prisons be constructed at the expense of the Church in order to punish those Indians who either taught or followed the doctrines of nagualism. In 1698, the Bishop notes:

All are not so subject to the promptings of the Devil as formerly, but there are still some so closely allied to him that they transform themselves into tigers, lions, bulls, flashes of light and globes of fire. We can say from the declaration and solemn confession of some penitents that it is proved that the Devil had carnal relations with them . . . approaching them in the form of their Nagual.[141]

It is interesting that the Bishop living in an earlier age had no doubts about the reality of the nagual or about the ability of the nagualists to transform themselves into animals, to become invisible, to travel in a second to distant places, or to "create before the eyes of the spectator a river, a tree, a house, or an animal, where none such existed."[142] And now Castaneda would have us take such transformations and crafts as seriously as did the Spanish Catholics in the sixteenth, seventeenth and eighteenth centuries, though now with respect rather than condemnation.[143]

The Ally

Carlos has his first meeting with the ally on September 3, 1969, when he uses don Juan's smoking mixture. He has a vision of a distant slope plowed in horizontal furrows. A man who appears to be a Mexican peasant comes toward him along one of the furrows. There are three boulders in the field, and at the bottom of the slope is a water canyon. The ally takes a string from a pouch he is carrying and wraps it around his left hand. A moment later, he points to the area in front of him. Don Juan interprets the experience to mean that Carlos has three major stumbling blocks on the path of knowledge, that he needs a spirit catcher like the string in the ally's pouch, and that he will draw his greatest powers from gullies or canyons such as the one pointed out by the ally.[144]

The ally is an experience available to all of us; it is not a strange spirit that inhabits the mountains of Mexico and that only such rare individuals as Carlos may meet. Jung has the following to say about the seeing of spirits:

> It is generally assumed that the seeing of apparitions is far commoner among primitives than among civilized people, the inference being that this is nothing but superstition, because civilized people do not have such visions unless they are ill. It is quite certain that civilized man makes much less use of the hypothesis of spirits than the primitive, but in my view it is equally certain that psychic phenomena occur no less frequently with civilized people than they do with primitives. The only difference is that where the primitive speaks of ghosts, the European speaks of dreams and fantasies and neurotic symptoms, and attributes less importance to them than the primitive does. I am convinced that if a European had to go through the same exercises and ceremonies which the medicine-man performs in order to make the spirits visible, he would have the same experiences. He would interpret them differently, of course, and devalue them, but this would not alter the facts as such.[145]

The ally is what we are accustomed to call a spirit. If we look at spirits and allies psychologically, writes Jung, they "are unconscious autonomous complexes which appear as projections because they have no direct association with the ego."[146] Jung also makes a distinction between souls and spirits based on the psychology of primitives. Both souls and spirits are unconscious autonomous complexes, but souls are felt to belong to the ego whereas spirits are alien. Accordingly, two types of illness are recognized in primitive psychology: loss of soul and possession by a spirit. Being depressed is an example of loss of soul, since it involves a loss of energy and interest that is otherwise available to consciousness. The appearance, however, of strange, erratic behavior or fits of rage would indicate a case of possession.[147]

Souls and spirits or allies are connected and are part of a psychological continuum. The same psychological factor will be experienced at the soul end of the continuum as personal, and at the spirit end as impersonal and alien. We can imagine this process in terms of an individual's anger as it appears in dreams. If the individual is cut off from his anger, he may experience an uncanny fear when in a situation that constellates his anger. Perhaps he dreams that there is some terrifying, unnamable force in the basement. Over time he begins to develop a relationship to his anger, and as he becomes more capable of integrating this aspect of his shadow, the representations of his anger in his dreams will undergo various transformations. The anger may appear as a raging bull that threatens him, later as the god of war, Ares. As the god Ares, his anger is in a recognizable human form but it is still impersonal, godlike, a potential ally but not yet wrestled to the ground. As his anger becomes a more natural part of his life he may dream of an angry friend. At the beginning of the process, he experienced anger as an uncanny, alien force, but eventually as a familiar part of himself. In the process of realization, of taming this ally, he may have uncovered major secrets concerning his life and his personal myth, because the ally is, as don Juan says, the "giver of secrets." The ally, of course, could just as well be love, creative energy, religious ideas or any other archetypal possibility.

The ally is a concept that evolves through various stages in Castaneda's work. In *The Teachings of Don Juan,* Carlos assumes that the power plants, the devil's weed and the little smoke, are don Juan's allies and may one day become his. In the second book, *A Separate Reality,* Carlos learns that the power plants are not allies but that they take one to where the ally can be found. Carlos again uses the little smoke and comes in contact with the ally in the form of a Mexican peasant. On another occasion he goes to meet the ally without the use of don Juan's smoking mixture. He is alone in the mountains at night when he hears branches cracking all around him. He spends the night curled up on the ground holding his midsection, while terrifying noises happen all around him and almost seem to attack his stomach.

At the end of *Journey to Ixtlan,* Carlos meets the ally in the form of a coyote, and he accomplishes the task without the use of the little smoke. Furthermore, the experience of the coyote-ally is not frightening; he and the coyote get along quite well and have a pleasant conversation. In *Tales of Power,* Carlos has an experience of what don Juan calls the true ally—a moth. After his encounter with the moth in the chaparral, he goes on to do active imagination and through active imagination to *see* his friends and acquaintances both in Los Angeles and Mexico. The final information on the ally thus far occurs in the encounters with the allies of don Juan and don Genaro, as reported in *Tales of Power* and *The Second Ring of Power.*

The ally was first projected onto the power plants and concretized as an external factor. Later, however, Carlos comes to see that the ally is an autonomous psychological factor independent of the hallucinogenic plants and capable of assuming any form. The form taken by the ally need not be a human form. One of don Juan's allies, for example, appears as a dark rectangular shape.

A woman I work with in analysis recently dreamed of an ally in the form of a filing cabinet. The cabinet behaved in a tricksterish way, eating her food, snapping her skirt off and continuing to follow her with impish tricks. At the bottom of the filing cabinet she discovered a series of photographs she had recently taken. Photography is now the dreamer's major creative outlet. The dream was saying that the various aspects of her life were too neatly filed away, compartmentalized; the unconscious was trying to disrupt her routines, but also showing her a way to express herself creatively. She subsequently dreamed of a mischievous man, behind her and her husband in the cinema, who kept tapping them on the shoulders. The latest appearance of this trickster was in a dream where she was talking with her husband. Her husband had an innocent expression on his face and was totally unaware of an imp on his shoulder making faces at his wife. This points to the fact that the dreamer's husband is unconscious of his own mischief in the relationship, but the dream series points to a problem they share, that of repressing too much life and denying their creative, individual instincts. Presumably, the unconscious ally will mischievously disrupt things until the dreamer takes up the problem of unlived life.

After having overvalued the power plants, Carlos uses the smoking mixture to meet the ally. The appearance of the ally as a Mexican peasant suggests the importance of the earthy, instinctive side of life that Carlos is divorced from. The ally seems to want a relationship with Carlos since he comes toward him and since he shows Carlos the means of building a relationship—the spirit catcher. Don Juan's comment about the ally showing Carlos that he will draw his greatest power from gullies and canyons is interesting in the light of La Gorda's revelation later that the vision of God or the "human mold" is associated with gullies. It would seem that this earthy ally leads Carlos to deeper spiritual experience and understanding.

I am both perplexed and fascinated with the connection between canyons and the experience of God. Different geological formations seem to suggest different psychological constellations or processes; the sacredness of places deserves more investigation. The gully or canyon in Carlos's vision is green in comparison to the arid mountain terrain that surrounds it. In such an environment perhaps canyons are places where life-giving water chooses to flow or to store itself, places where one can imagine the possibility of something coming out of nothing. God, La Gorda says, is an imaginable "entity" that groups together the force of life into a human shape out of the teeming emptiness of the nagual.[148] By way of comparison, the Greeks located their places of contact with the gods around sacred groves and springs.

Next, Carlos experiences the ally in the mountains at night as a terrifying auditory and physical presence. The ally does not take a visible shape, and thus the experience is alien and cannot be related to his knowledge of himself or of the world. He hears branches cracking all around him, then slurping sounds, squeaking sounds and the sounds of wings flapping above him while he is in a foetal position on the ground. Many of these sounds he experiences as physical sensations. Near the end of this nightmarish experience he feels something soft tapping him on the back of the neck.

Carlos's experience here is reminiscent of such poltergeist phenomena as moving objects, strange sounds and unexplainable lights. Such phenomena belong to the extreme end of the spectrum of exteriorized complexes. As William G. Roll's research has shown, poltergeist phenomena are always associated with a specific individual.[149] When that individual is not present, the bizarre parapsychological events do not occur. He was able to give psychological tests to a number of individuals who were associated with cases of such parapsychological phenomena, and in each case he found that the individual was quite complex-ridden, with a high level of inner stress. His research confirms Jung's much earlier assertion of the connection between parapsychological events and a highly charged emotional complex split off from the conscious awareness of the individual involved.

An analysand of mine once had an experience strikingly similar to Carlos's with the ally. He had gone alone on a fishing trip in the mountains, and contrary to habit he chose to explore an unfamiliar part of the river terrain. While sitting in front of the fire, like Carlos he began to have an invading and unnerving fantasy about a mean, rugged sort of man coming up behind and hitting him on the neck or back of the head. While gripped by the fantasy, a branch suddenly and inexplicably broke off from the tree overhead and fell precisely on the back of his neck. This isolated place and the synchronistic event of the broken branch suggest the presence of the ally. This particular individual was threatened by his own aggressive masculine shadow. Normally it remained in the psychological background, but when he was separated from his familiar environment, the complex emerged and threatened to overwhelm him from outside.

In *Journey to Ixtlan,* Carlos experiences the ally in the form of a coyote. The coyote is a familiar representation of the archetype of the trickster. Tricksters are typically up to some nonsense, but in the process of their foolishness and mischief they also bring new things to consciousness. The coyote in Native American mythology is the one who brings sense out of nonsense and culture out of chaos, even though it is chaos of his own making. He is also an expression of the wisdom, growth and insight that comes in the wake of an individual's willingness to follow the seeming foolishness of the unconscious. I think no one would be surprised to find that Castaneda has a trickster ally.

Carlos's ability to talk with the coyote and have an intelligible conversation is a familiar motif in myth and fairytale, where heroes and heroines often have animal teachers and helpers. Shamans throughout the world likewise have animal spirits as guides and helpers, and in their apprenticeship they often learn the language of animals. This motif expresses the individual's ability to comprehend the instinctive or animal levels of the psyche. In fact, in the Native American tradition many hunters received their power from a specific animal ally who would appear in dreams or visions. The animals were also observed in waking life and their habits and ways often imitated. The animal spirits taught men and women how to live and also could tell the hunter where to find game when game was scarce.

Next, in *Tales of Power,* Carlos experiences the ally as a moth. Carlos and don Juan go to a power spot in the chaparral not far from don Juan's ramada. There in the darkness don Juan has Carlos sit facing the southeast and stop his internal dialogue. When he is able to stop the internal dialogue that supports the tonal or conscious view of the world, he isolates a silhouette in the darker background of the bushes. The tonal is still sufficiently present for Carlos to want to identify the silhouette as that of a man. The objective observer in Carlos, however, is intact enough to allow the shape to take its own form. At this moment he experiences pain in his stomach, and when he releases the tension, he sees the dark outline of a large bird fly at him from the bushes. Carlos screams and falls on his back.

Immediately don Juan and Carlos walk in silence back to the ramada. Don Juan explains to him that his tonal put together the image of a man. Don Juan says that the dark shape was actually a moth, though even this statement is not the final truth but only a way of speaking. Moths, he explains, are "the guardians of eternity ... the depositories of the gold dust of eternity."[150] The knowledge that a warrior seeks is the gold dust that comes floating down like a shower from the wings of the moth. Don Juan tells Carlos that the moth has a call, and that if he is able to stop the internal dialogue and attend to the moth's call, he will be able to *see*. Carlos experiences the sound as a physical sensation. The sputtering sound brings with it the memory of the laughter of his stepson. He indulges in the memory until don Juan brings him out of his trance. Don Juan also takes the hint from Carlos's memory and explains that the task set for him this night is to *see* all of his friends. As Carlos attends to the moth's call, "spherical bubbles" float toward him, bubbles like gold dust. The bubbles break one by one, and each reveals a scene to him that enables him to *see* the people he has selected from among his friends.

The appearance of the ally as a moth signifies that Carlos has come a long way. The ally is no longer a threatening figure but rather a beautiful creature of the night. At the heart of the symbol of the moth is the process of transformation. The moth is a fascinating creature that begins as a caterpillar, builds a cocoon, then transforms into a pupa from which comes a beautiful winged being that seeks the light. The moth is the transformative aspect of the unconscious that seeks to enter consciousness. It is the secret transformation that wants to happen in the life of a warrior. Another way to express this is to say that the ally is the secret of transformation revealed through active imagination.

The moth's call is what Jeff Raff, an analyst in Denver, has called a "threshold phenomenon" of active imagination. A "threshold phenomenon" is usually an auditory or physical event that occurs just at the moment when one's consciousness is making the transition from the waking state into the unconscious. The "threshold phenomenon" signals the transition, but it also frequently surprises the person doing active imagination and snaps the person back into the waking state.

The image of knowledge as gold dust descending from the wings of a moth expresses a new development in Carlos's work with active imagination. Formerly he approached the unconscious with the fear of one who is prepared for combat. Now he is capable of experiencing the nagual with an attitude of active receptivity.

There is a parallel to this image of knowledge as gold dust in the Greek myth of Danae and Zeus.[151] Akrisios, the king of Argos, had one child from his marriage, a girl named Danae. This perfect child grows to be a perfect woman. The king wants a son and inquires of the oracle at Delphi. The oracle replies that he will never have a son but that his daughter shall, and that her son will be his downfall. Akrisios returns from Delphi and builds a bronze chamber in the palace and shuts his daughter inside with a maid. Danae is such an exceptional woman, however, that she attracts the attention of Zeus. Zeus transforms himself into golden rain that descends through the roof and into the underground chamber. The maid catches the golden rain in her garment, and from the gold dust Zeus emerges. Danae's prison becomes a marriage chamber, and out of this sacred union Danae gives birth to the Greek hero Perseus.

Zeus as a psychological experience is equivalent to the moment of illumination.[152] The moment of illumination is the moment of knowledge, and the gold dust is the "treasure hard to obtain." The story of Danae and Zeus adds the element of a sacred union to the quest for knowledge. Carlos is now the receptive bride of knowledge rather than the warrior seeking to claim knowledge. Carlos is in a position to be pregnant with this new knowledge, that is, to produce something new and real out of the union.

In terms of the evolution of the concept of the ally, Carlos's experience with the moth reveals that the true ally, the "giver of secrets," is active imagination itself.[153] The moth symbolizes the liberation of consciousness, transformed from an earthbound to a winged existence. Active imagination is the liberation of consciousness from the bounds of ordinary time and space. Carlos's encounter with the moth is the culmination of our understanding of the essential nature of the ally. Although the ally is an archetypal complex, even more fundamentally it is the process of active imagination itself.

Much later Carlos meets the allies of don Juan and don Genaro. The allies of don Juan are experienced as a dark rectangular shadow and a coyote, while the allies of don Genaro are a jaguar and a "long-faced, bald-headed, extraordinarily tall, glowing man." We are already familiar with the coyote ally. The jaguar is a symbol of the shaman's affinity with and journey to the underworld. According to B.C. Brundage in *The Fifth Sun,* the same Mayan word, *balam,* is used for jaguar and sorcerer.[154] The jaguar is especially linked to Tezcatlipoca, the dark shamanic god of the Aztecs. Brundage describes Tezcatlipoca as "an invisible and omniextensive god, a sorcerer, a trickster, a manic, a seer and a shape shifter."[155] The Aztecs likewise perceived the jaguar itself as a seer:

> It is a dweller of the forests, of crags, of water; noble, princely, it is said. It is the lord, the ruler of animals. It is cautious, wise, proud. It is not a scavenger. It is one which detests, which is nauseated by dirty things. It is noble, proud.... And by night it watches; it seeks out what it hunts, what it eats. Very good, clear is its vision. In truth, it sees very well; it can see far. Even if it is very dark, even if it is misty, it sees.[156]

The jaguar symbolizes the consciousness that prowls and stalks in the darkness and the mists of the other world. The jaguar becomes human in the warrior who *sees* and who stalks the knowledge and fulfilment of his or her myth.

The trickster-hero and the shaman-hero are both archetypal complexes that exist independently of don Juan and don Genaro. The dark shadow and the bald-headed man are less defined; consequently their psychological configuration is difficult to assess, though we can assume that both symbolize archetypal shadow qualities. We are told that the allies are attracted to Carlos's luminosity. Presumably these archetypal complexes will stand in a similar relation to Carlos as they once did to don Juan, and will continue to try to become conscious through Carlos.

To amplify the concept of the ally I will mention a woman's relationship to a male ally. The woman is thirty and extremely gifted, but she has lived a provisional life, only marginally able to commit herself to her own process. She first dreamed of her ally, a colorfully eccentric and wise Englishman, three years ago. After a relationship developed with this man in her dreams, she began to seek him out occasionally in dreams and active imagination. Depressed and unhappy, she dreamed one evening that she went to visit him:

> I go looking for L.S. I go to his house and knock on the door. A woman housekeeper, middle-aged and very chipper, very British, answers. "Oh," she says, "you're just in time to catch him. It's the Day of Costumes, you know."
>
> She steps back and a bunch of people come out in vivid shining costumes. They go past me out the door. Last comes L.S., and his

costume almost makes me scream. His clothes are dark, vague, but he wears whiteface, and his face is made up to look like a pig. It's terrifying. He has a light blue ribbon around his neck and a straw hat with a fake flower sticking out of it on his head. It's very ludicrousness makes it more frightening. He is the last person on earth I want to see looking this way. Yet something of beauty looks at me out of his eyes. "It's the Day of Costumes," he says, "remember that." Then he says, "You're sick. I can help you. If you can look *into* my face, you can establish a direct relationship with the beyond."

I am terrified of his pig-face but I force myself to look at him. I look right into his eyes. His eyes and the area around them dissolve into perfectly clear light—all that remains are little black lines to mark the edge of his pupils and the outline of his eyelids. But the rest is clear, colorless, full of light, clearer than clear water, and seems to me infinite. It makes me dizzy. Then, gradually the light clouds a little, and his eyes fill in and return. Once again I'm looking into his face.

"You see?" he says.

Her ally's eyes recall the water of the eyes of Mescalito, the eyes of the unconscious. Her ally is a combination of a mercurial trickster and a wise old man. He loosens up all of the guilt-ridden tightness of her conscious attitude with his costumes; he connects her to the mysterious waters of the unconscious, and perhaps he even shows her here that it is acceptable to be a pig and want more out of life than she dares to ask. Although her ally has appeared in different bodies and disguises, his name and highly specific personality always remain the same. Although intellectually it seems appropriate to speak of this figure and of the ally as an archetypal complex, feeling has a different response and willingly acknowledges the ally's independent life and existence outside our limits of space and time.

This woman's ally has consistently revealed to her profound truths and insights, and has been a reliable guide in the right way for her to live. Her relationship with him has also gradually become more grounded. Several months after the above dream, she dreamed her ally arrived for the first time in America; the distance separating the conscious attitude of the dreamer from that of her ally had lessened. And not long ago, she dreamed that she was to marry this English gentleman. When she awoke from the dream, she knew immediately that she would no longer be able to evade the responsibility to fulfill her task in life, by running away or committing suicide. The marriage with her ally was like a marriage to her own individuation process, and in this, as in other ways, the ally has become a very real aspect of her everyday life.

We have seen the ally as an autonomous spirit or complex that may appear in any conceivable form—a Mexican peasant, a coyote, a jaguar, a moth, etc. Ultimately, the allies are the masks of God.

The ally is an aspect of God that forces itself upon us in dreams, visions, symptoms, and uncanny synchronistic events. The allies are God's attempts at incarnation, at becoming conscious through us. Behind our struggles with the allies are the distant echoes of Jacob wrestling with the angel and Job insisting on justice in the face of Yahweh's irascibility.[157] There is nothing more noble, terrifying or transforming for humankind than this encounter with the "giver of secrets."

Having encountered the moth ally in active imagination, Carlos now has rounded up his "second attention" sufficiently to be capable of true shamanic flight.

The Leap into the Nagual

At the edge of a cliff Carlos stands between don Juan and don Genaro. Don Juan begins whispering in his right ear while don Genaro whispers in Carlos's left ear. The teacher and the benefactor whisper respectively of the tonal and the nagual. Carlos then has the sensation of being tossed into the void. The "me" that he knows disintegrates into a thousand pieces. He knows at that moment that the thousand pieces are his separate awarenesses. They constitute the "colony" that comes together to form himself. Periodically something stirs all these scattered "nuggets of awareness," and the life force brings them back together in the awareness that Carlos knows as "myself." At those times, Carlos witnesses a coherent scene of the everyday world or a coherent scene of the nagual. On one of these occasions Carlos witnesses the scene of himself and don Juan at the top of the cliff. He experiences this scene as real, physical, and in the next moment don Juan reaches over and hugs him.[158]

When don Juan and don Genaro whisper into Carlos's right and left ears respectively, they are performing the act they call splitting the apprentice. The actual moment is the summation of the teachings Carlos has struggled with from the beginning of his apprenticeship. He has learned to focus his attention on conscious life and clean his particular island of the tonal. This is symbolized by don Juan whispering in Carlos's right ear. He has also learned to focus his "second attention" on the nagual, and his benefactor don Genaro now directs that attention through his whisperings. The act of focusing one's attention on both worlds liberates one's consciousness from exclusive attachment to either world. Thus when he is tossed into the void he is able to witness scenes of both the tonal and the nagual, including the scene with himself on top of the cliff. This liberated consciousness is the psychic mid-point that ideally emerges during the journey on the path of knowledge or individuation. The experience of this new form of consciousness brings with it the recognition of the truth of don Juan's assertion that "we are perceivers." We are perceivers who may witness many worlds without absolute bondage to any one of them.

Carlos's experience of the disintegration of his awareness into separate particles, and the subsequent reunion of those particles, tells us something further about the nature of consciousness. Our consciousness is made up of a plurality of souls, of independently functioning units of consciousness. We can easily recognize this fact in terms of our thinking, feeling, sensation, intuition, instinctive responses, and so on, but Carlos carries this plurality further. Let us imagine that in one moment we are observing something with our eyes while at the same time following a quite unrelated train of thought, while at the same time experiencing some sensation in our knees, while at the same time noticing that we are feeling something in our knees, and so on in a continually changing arrangement of consciousnesses from moment to moment. In the account of Carlos's leap, we see all these separate awarenesses going separate ways. These nuggets are held together, however, by the guardian spirit on the side of the tonal and by the will on the side of the nagual. Carlos has learned to trust this instinctive cohesiveness of his individuality. Most people legitimately fear that a profound experience of the unconscious could lead to disintegration, and thus the guardian is encouraged to become a more vigilant guard. The warrior, however, organizes his life and tunes his will to such a degree that he can experience himself as the one and the many.

The accounts of shamans reveal the same pattern of dismemberment and restitution. In Siberia, for instance, the shaman's observing ego witnesses the death, dismemberment and restoration of the body and is required to learn the names of all the different bones and organs in the shaman's language. After the bones have been cooked and cleaned, they are replaced, although in some accounts the bones are replaced by metal bones signifying the solidity and endurance of the shaman's restructured personality. The shaman is forced to experience the fragmentariness of his own consciousness, to differentiate the complexities of his nature, and this experience is forced on him often by his own psychological breakdown.

In the shaman's dream or trance, he does not restore himself but rather witnesses this work being done by the ancestor shaman or shamans. The ancestor shaman symbolizes the unconscious urge toward individuation (the will) that is equally responsible for his breakdown and for his reconstitution. Like Carlos, the shaman is taught to trust in the innate wisdom of the unconscious.

The Double

When Carlos reflects on his leap into the nagual, described above, he realizes that he has two very distinct memories—the memory of the continuous series of scenes that he witnessed interspersed by moments of disintegration, and the continuous memory of being at the top of the cliff clowning with don Genaro. With these two uninterrupted memories, it dawns on Carlos that they are memories of two experiences that were happening at the same time.

Don Juan reminds Carlos of an earlier leap, when his consciousness disappeared from the edge of the cliff and plummeted to the bottom of the ravine below. While at the bottom, don Genaro threw a rock from the top of the cliff down into the ravine. Don Juan reminds Carlos that he had a memory of seeing don Genaro throw the rock and a memory of being at the bottom of the ravine seeing the rock tumbling down. The Carlos that is seeing don Genaro throw the rock is the Carlos we know. The Carlos at the bottom of the ravine is the double. The double is the subtle body that exists in the unconscious.

The double, don Juan says, is developed through *dreaming;* or more correctly, one becomes aware of the double in the process of *dreaming.* The double is the awareness of our luminosity, according to don Juan. We can interpret his statements to mean that through dream analysis, *dreaming,* active imagination and other forms of work on the unconscious, we become aware of the larger personality that exists in us. This larger personality is oneself, and yet it is more than we are capable of realizing in the realm of the tonal regardless of how much the ego self and the double begin to approximate each other. As the awareness of our luminosity, the double is the awareness of our totality that is both personal and suprapersonal, sacred and profane. The double is the "I" that witnesses and experiences the vaster realms of vision. The subtle body of active imagination does not experience the same limitations of time and space imposed upon us in waking life.

We can amplify the double with the Taoist alchemical text concerning immortality, *The Secret of The Golden Flower.* Here we find the following: "When the One note of individuation enters into birth, essence and life are divided into two. From this time on, if the utmost peace is not achieved, essence and life never see each other again."[159]

We recognize that the terms "essence" and "life" relate specifically to the double and the waking self, and more generally to the nagual and the tonal. For the Taoist, the practice of the "backward flowing method" involves deep introspection and yogic practices that lead to the appearance of the subtle body, the experience and awareness of one's "essence."

> The Light is easy to move, but difficult to fix. If it is allowed to go long enough in a circle, then it crystallizes itself; that is the natural spirit-body.... It is the condition of which is said in the Book of the Seal of the Heart: Silently in the morning thou fliest upward.[160]

The double holds the secret of true shamanic flight and the transcendence of our mortality, according to don Juan, the Taoists and other religious traditions.

Don Juan remarks to Carlos that a moment arrives when the warrior becomes conscious of the paradox behind the experience of the waking self and the double. The paradox is that as much as it seems that the waking self dreams the double, it is also true that the double dreams the waking self. In his autobiography, Jung refers to a dream he had about this problem of "the dreamer and the dreamed." In the dream he entered a "small wayside chapel," on the altar of which was a "wonderful flower arrangement" in place of the crucifix and the image of the Virgin Mary. In front of the altar, he saw a yogi "in lotus posture, in deep meditation." He was shocked to see that the yogi had his face, and the shock awoke him with the thought, "Aha, so he is the one who is meditating me. He has a dream, and I am it. I knew that when he awakened, I would no longer be."[161] Jung says of the dream:

> The figure of the yogi, then, would more or less represent my unconscious prenatal wholeness, and the Far East, as is often the case in dreams, a psychic state alien and opposed to our own.... the yogi's meditation "projects" my empirical reality.[162]

From the point of view of the ego, it would seem that we dream the double in the process of attempting to become conscious of our wholeness, while from the point of view of the double, it would seem that the double dreams us in order to actualize itself in "three-dimensional existence." Like Jung's dream, Carlos's experience of the double "suggests that in the opinion of the 'other side,' our unconscious existence is the real one and our conscious world a kind of illusion, an apparent reality constructed for a specific purpose, like a dream which seems a reality as long as we are in it."[163]

Later in Chapter Six we will return to the issue of the survival after death of individual consciousness in the form of the double. But first we will look at the special problems raised by Castaneda's fifth book, *The Second Ring of Power*.

6

Trials and Revelations

It has been two years since Carlos said goodbye to don Juan and don Genaro and made his leap into the abyss from the barren mountaintop in central Mexico. Carlos returns now to visit Pablito and Nestor and to seek their understanding of the compelling visions he experienced in that leap. On an impulse he stops in the marketplace of the city where he was accustomed to meet don Juan. His body feels don Juan's presence, and later, with equal certainty his body feels that don Juan has left. The next morning Carlos drives several hours to Pablito's house. He is greeted by Pablito's mother, donna Soledad, who, unlike the tired, obese woman he had once known, now appears younger and more vital, with a trim, muscular body. Through his encounter with donna Soledad, Carlos realizes that don Juan and don Genaro have left this world and that for the first time he is alone on his path, unable to turn to don Juan for guidance or warmth. The apprenticeship is over.[164]

Donna Soledad, like the "little sisters" after her, was instructed by don Juan to steal Carlos's power for use on her own journey, and if necessary, to kill him. Donna Soledad draws upon a wide array of ploys to seduce Carlos and to rob him of his power. After all attempts have failed, she finally talks with him at length with the private knowledge that he is vulnerable to words. She talks with him about herself, about the "little sisters," about how they all became apprenticed to don Juan and about their individual struggles. When she has drawn Carlos nearer to her with words, she uses her chance to grab him with her headband, pulls him abruptly to her and attempts to strangle him. While Carlos is about to suffocate, his nagual emerges. He becomes aware that he is looking down at his limp body on the bed being held fiercely around the neck by donna Soledad, and he reacts by striking her with a strong blow to the forehead. After this attack from Carlos's double, donna Soledad is powerless to cause further harm, and when she regains consciousness she fears that she has lost her soul.[166]

Without a Guide

Although don Juan is no longer of this world, his presence is still felt in the complex challenges that Carlos and the other apprentices have to face. Don Juan has left behind a complicated set of instructions for the various apprentices, drawing them into battle with each other but also into a deeper sense of unity. *The Second Ring of Power,* Castaneda's fifth book, describes the events of several days, during which Carlos experiences succeeding waves of disturbing realizations, first with the women apprenticed to don Juan and then with the men apprenticed to don Genaro.

Carlos's first and deepest shock is his encounter with donna Soledad, whom he is surprised to find was an apprentice to don Juan even prior to his arrival in 1961. After surviving the battle with donna Soledad, Carlos moves on to similar struggles with Lidia, Rosa, Josefina—don Juan's apprentices and donna Soledad's wards. Only when he is able to survive the battles of power with donna Soledad and the "little sisters" does he meet La Gorda, the most impeccable warrior of the nine and the one who most closely resembles don Juan in her mastery of herself and her circumstances. Subsequently, Carlos is reunited with his friends and companions, Pablito, Nestor and Benigno, the apprentices of don Genaro. This small community of nine women and men can then begin to explore their complex internal relationships and their common bond. Carlos gives us a precise description of the realm of experience he has entered:

> Don Juan's apprentices were not in any way as engulfing as he was. Their revelations, although extraordinary, were only missing pieces to a jigsaw puzzle. The unusual character of those pieces was that with them the picture did not become clearer but that it became more and more complex.[165]

The world of *The Second Ring of Power* is more complex than the one we experienced in the first four books; for the first time we do not have don Juan's explanations or presence to realign and center us. Carlos is on his own, surrounded by equals. Although Carlos may have balked at the authority of don Juan and don Genaro, he was nonetheless comfortable in their authority. Now he has no place to rest, and neither as readers do we. We can no longer turn to don Juan as in the other books, and to make matters worse, we have nine different points of view, all to be taken seriously. We experience radically different, conflicting feelings from the nine apprentices about don Juan, don Genaro and about each other. For instance, Carlos experiences La Gorda as an impeccable warrior and as a woman he can trust, but when Pablito arrives at the house, he will not speak with Carlos until he gets rid of La Gorda, calling her "that witch." Pablito refers to Carlos affectionately as "the maestro," but elsewhere Carlos is described by some of the women as a "devil" and as someone incapable of showing respect or affection.

Since we have nine different people, we have to be prepared to look at any experience from nine different points of view. We cannot rest only in trying to understand what the purpose of Carlos's encounter with donna Soledad is for Carlos; we must also see what it means for her and what the implications are for the other seven apprentices. Only in this way can we adequately arrive at the meaning that this book may have for us and for our own journey. Finally, like Carlos, we have to stand on our own feet and make our own judgments now, without the support of don Juan.

The Second Ring of Power is concerned with what occurs when the teacher is gone, when the apprentice no longer has a master on whom to rely. In this case, inner authority must replace the relation to the teacher. Each of the nine apprentices is confronted with this challenge to integrate the teachings of don Juan and don Genaro, and to discover and rely upon their own inner resources. Also, eight of the apprentices (Donna Soledad is excluded because she must go off alone) find that their task in life binds them to each other. They learn that their fates are intertwined and that they must follow the instructions left by don Juan and don Genaro to live harmoniously together.

The apprentices thus far have not been able to sustain a positive relationship to the opposite sex. The men and the women of this book do not get along. They have a basis of community in their warrior's task and in their commitment to building a relationship to the nagual, but at this point the bonds of affection and trust that exist among them do not extend to the opposite sex. Carlos finds the community split, and as warriors they are challenged to heal this division. The wholeness they are seeking must become manifest in the experience of fulfilment in community. The community in itself symbolizes wholeness insofar as there are four women and four men. Four is the number of wholeness or completion and of balance and harmony; eight symbolizes the realization of the quality of four at a more evolved level; in other words, eight points toward a more differentiated experience of totality.

As implied in the powerful connection between these four women and four men, *The Second Ring of Power* is concerned with the differentiation of feminine and masculine values and modes of experience, and thus with differentiated relationships. Judging from the events in the book, the apprentices have a long way to go before they are capable of genuine eros. For all their shortcomings, the apprentices do have something to teach us. Our own relationships with the opposite sex are bedeviled by power struggles more often than we would like to admit, and although our power struggles may seem less magical, they are certainly no less lethal and no less sophisticated. We may learn something about our own predicament by closely examining the attempts and the failures at relationship of these apprentices.

In Carlos's battles with donna Soledad and the "little sisters," his victories are also defeats and their defeats are also victories. Each battle paves the way for possible relationship. Carlos's victory over donna Soledad is the defeat of his false innocence and of his habitual unwillingness to commit himself to authentic experience. Both tendencies thwart the possibility of genuine relatedness. Similarly, donna Soledad's power opposes the experience of eros. Her defeat is the victory of vulnerability over power. Donna Soledad's strength is not destroyed but rather made more complete by the acceptance of vulnerability. Thus, while *The Second Ring of Power* suffers in many ways from the absence of eros, it does suggest the possibility and the means of growing beyond the limitations of the role identifications that are no longer tenable when one is required to love.

In talking about *The Second Ring of Power* with Allen Ashby in 1978, we decided it would be appropriate for us as readers to set up a test for Carlos. We asked ourselves what we would need to see in the next book or books to determine that Carlos is not spinning further and further away from the earth. We wanted a test that would put us at ease with the question of whether or not this man was still worth following. We decided that for us to take Carlos seriously in the future, we would have to be convinced that he was making his best attempt to fulfill don Juan's last recommendation at the end of *Tales of Power,* namely to find a deep love of the earth. Psychologically, a love of the earth would show up as a deep sense of satisfaction with life and especially as affection, warmth and respect among these eight apprentices.

If Castaneda is writing fiction and if he remains unconscious and ungripped by what he is writing, then he is more likely to become caught up in the miraculous and magical aspects of the unconscious. We would then expect to find him becoming less and less human. If, however, Castaneda is writing roughly factual material or if he is writing complete fiction but still trying to integrate the path of knowledge into his life, then he would be compelled to love the earth, his life and his companions. We would expect him to become more richly human and to find a connection to the spirit that would transform his everyday life. In essence, the test we felt it would be reasonable to set for Carlos was to see whether or not he learns to love and respect his companions. If Carlos and the other apprentices do not learn to love, then we can assume that at some point they have wandered from the path of knowledge.

The Roots of the Devil's Weed

As we have seen in the episode with La Catalina, it is not totally unlike don Juan to set up Carlos, and by implication the other apprentices, for a potentially lethal battle. Carlos was set up with La Catalina as his worthy opponent in order to force him to use all that he had learned and to choose to remain an apprentice. Carlos is again at a crossroads, and don Juan has again fallen into the shadow of his power—succumbed to the temptation of every sorcerer, teacher, guide or therapist to manipulate and control events. The fact of don Juan's plot, however, does not invalidate the significance and the meaning of the battle between these two warriors who have become worthy opponents for each other. Deadly power struggles are common enough between sorcerers in the literature of shamanism. Looking further into this particular struggle illumines the nature of many of our own conflicts with power.

When Carlos sees donna Soledad step out of her house and come to greet him, he is surprised to find that she is no longer a "helpless old woman" with the shape of a "pyramid." Instead, she is physically trim and vigorous and her demeanor is bold and sexual. She has been transformed. As Carlos's awareness of her transformation penetrates deeper, he is profoundly affected. He sees her as though for the first time, and the result of his new awareness is the realization that he must look at all of his companions in a new light. Donna Soledad's transformation will spin and reorient Carlos. He must reexamine his world and acknowledge his blindness to the people around him, and in particular his blindness to women. Later, La Gorda will explain to Carlos that his encounter with donna Soledad was an omen revealing that women, not men, would for a while now be his teachers. Furthermore, the experience will show him the ways in which women are ahead of men in the quest for knowledge.

If we disregard for a moment the witchcraft in the meeting with donna Soledad, we see that this pattern shows up repeatedly in people's lives. Major transitions for both men and women are often brought about or accompanied by an encounter with someone of the opposite sex. For instance, a man in the middle of his life may find that his attention and energy want to go elsewhere than along the well-trodden paths, and that this change in his life is affected by the presence of a real woman. The new person constellates the need for transformation. If, on the other hand, the man is attuned to the inner life, it is just as likely that the transformation will come about through the trend of his own unconscious feminine nature. The inner woman appears as a personification of the unconscious and turns his eyes in another direction. She may appear in his dreams, for instance, as a painter, a gardener or a poet, anticipating the new developments in his own life which he begins to explore as he paints, tends a garden or writes. The new developments will lead in unexpected ways to the deepening of the personality and a richer vision.

We will come to the specific nature of Carlos's transformation later; for now, we will return to the first tense moments of Carlos's meeting with donna Soledad. His body quickly begins to react to her, making him aware that she is a witch and that he is being entrapped. With this awareness, his strongest impulse is to leave; consequently, donna Soledad's greatest need is to hold him, to keep him from leaving. This particular constellation is quite common in relationships and just as often the sex roles are reversed. With this purpose in mind she employs stratagems to throw him off balance and to trap his attention. As soon as she has exhausted one ploy, she attempts another. Her tricks are the finest expression of manipulative skill. She appeals to his feeling, she distracts him, she challenges his masculine ego, she declares her good intentions, she invokes don Juan's authority to discredit Carlos and throw him off guard, and she uses unpredictable emotional behavior to disorient him. The list goes on. She tries sexual seduction, she uses guilt, she argues that fate has brought them together, she tries to gain his compliance by being understanding. Her most subtle ploy is to seduce Carlos with information, stories. When her trump card fails, she tries to strangle Carlos with her headband.

Donna Soledad's witchcraft, as we have just seen, is similar to something we are all familiar with—the semiconscious plotting that goes on in relationships and takes the form of: "If I do this, then he'll do that." Were Carlos more familiar with his own unconscious plots, then he would recognize the plots of others and be less surprised and frightened by donna Soledad's behavior. Her attempts to entrap Carlos constitute a glorious performance, and with an understanding of such plots, her use of every ploy to its utmost becomes humorous. When we are engaged in such plots, everything is calculated for its effect, and there is always a secret purpose.

While I was working on this material I heard a fine example of such unconscious plotting. A woman wanted to give a going-away party for a friend. She had a slight unresolved grievance with her friend, and because she failed to deal with her hurt and anger, she included among the guests, *without thinking,* two friends of hers who were openly hostile to the guest of honor. The two friends ultimately ruined the atmosphere of the party, and although her anger was satisfied unconsciously, she and the guests were wounded by the experience. Unconscious deviousness is equally at work when men behave in predictable ways to entangle and seduce or to foil and frustrate women. Such plots are experienced as though they were arranged and worked out by another personality because the conscious ego participates so peripherally in the design. Our plots function best in darkness; we on the other hand function best when we are aware of our own and others' plots.

Because Carlos relies so heavily on his intellect, and because of the lack of eros that we have already seen in the earlier books, we can assume that Carlos is not on the best of terms with either his own emotionally determined designs or with those of women. It is easy to believe that don Juan told donna Soledad that Carlos liked women and so would be an easy prey for her. We have seen Carlos an easy prey for women twice before—first with the devil's weed and secondly with La Catalina. The roots of the devil's weed produce sexual passion and physical vigor for the goal of power, not love. Donna Soledad's behavior has all of the characteristics of the roots of the devil's weed; she uses her sexuality and her strength to entrap. When she says that she and Carlos are one sexually, she is saying that they are identical in their unconsciousness of the split between power and love. Both must say "no" to this form of relationship— one through defeat and the other through victory. The notion of being one reappears later with La Gorda when she tells Carlos that they will one day be the same.[167] The unity that La Gorda and Carlos are moving toward, however, is of a different kind, characterized by warmth and respect.

It is interesting to look at the moment of donna Soledad's appeal to Carlos to "mix" sexually and become one. Carlos reacts to her appeal in a most unpredictable, effective and humorous manner. When this attractive woman stretches out on the bed and offers herself sexually, Carlos unexpectedly shouts, "But you're Pablito's mother!" and then he yells at the top of his lungs for don Juan. This is definitely an unusual response to seduction, but it must be said that such sudden, unexpected behavior is just the way to stop a hostile plot, a threatening animal or an attack of the nagual. Donna Soledad jumps from the bed and covers herself quickly with her skirt. Contrary to Carlos's bias for understanding, it is just his irrationality that again and again comes to his rescue.

Donna Soledad's Floor

While Carlos is in donna Soledad's bedroom, he notices that the original dirt floor he had once seen has been replaced by a floor made of fired reddish clay slabs. The slabs have been arranged in a symmetrical pattern with the lines originating from the north, donna Soledad's direction, and converging at the center of the room where her bed is placed. We know three additional things about the floor and its design. First, we know that with the help of don Juan and of the north wind, donna Soledad constructed the floor and then used the lines of the floor to make her young. She tells Carlos that she would lie in her bed and empty herself of all thoughts and feelings, and that as she did this, the lines of the floor would pull her wrinkles away. Secondly, donna Soledad had hoped that the power of the lines of the floor would weaken Carlos, but his attention and inspection of the floor and his excitement about the work disarmed its power. Finally, we know that as a result of her defeat in battle with Carlos, she will have to dismantle her floor and go off on her own in a direction different from that of Carlos and the other apprentices.

The design of the floor is obviously symbolic. It is a mandala, and as a mandala it has an integrating and centering effect. Because the lines are symmetric and converge at a center, the floor is a symbolic statement of the integration of donna Soledad's personality on a new level and of the creation of a new center to her personality. Furthermore, the convergence of the lines from the north—symbolically the area of the unconscious—shows us the psychological source of her transformation. (A discussion of the meaning of the wind as a factor involved in renewal will follow later in this chapter.)

Donna Soledad's bed is placed at the center where the lines converge. The bed's location at the center suggests that symbolically the bed is intimately connected with the reorganization of donna Soledad's life. In the past her adaptation to life was exclusively that of mothering. Being identified with the role of mother implies that sexuality is associated with children, not with pleasure or intimacy. Carlos's image of donna Soledad from the past confirms that she carried her identification with the mother role to the point of being a dedicated martyr. The position of the bed on the floor shows us that donna Soledad's awareness of her sexuality has been a central transforming factor in her development as a woman and as a warrior. Her sexuality, once ignored along with her body, is now part of her personal path and identity.

When a woman is identified exclusively with the role of mother, then her individual personality—symbolically, the body—is diminished and one sees only the role. In addition, when the mother role dominates, other people and even objects become children to be cared for. The individuality of the woman and that of the other person suffer because of the limitation of vision within the role: everyone and everything that is not mother becomes child.

As the mother-martyr, donna Soledad had considerable power, albeit unrecognized. Unconscious power is exercised unconsciously, usually through manipulation. With the construction of the floor and with her relationship to the north wind, there is a transformation in donna Soledad and in her sense of her own power. She now has sexual and personal power, and this is a tremendous advance in her development as a woman. There is still something missing, however, and it is the experience of love.

We definitely do not get the impression that donna Soledad is capable of intimacy. For this reason, she must lose the battle and dismantle her floor. The floor represents the integration of her personality on a new and higher level, but it is still not enough. The existing order—the floor—has to be destroyed and replaced by an integration that will contain and express more of who she is in her totality. I imagine that the new integration would include the bed as a central experience, but this time as a setting for intimacy rather than power. Donna Soledad had hoped that the newly acquired strength of her personality, symbolized by the design on her floor, would trap Carlos, but his attention and genuine interest must have touched just what was missing: her heart. No matter how unconsciously, he must have reached her vulnerability and thereby diminished the thrust of her aggression. She was shattered by his interest and by his refusal to submit to something beneath them both.

The creation and destruction of symbolic patterns of wholeness is a frequent theme in the process of individuation. Von Franz comments on this in *Individuation in Fairytales:*

> People may draw mandalas of some kind and you have the feeling that in their active imagination they are dwelling in this mandala. You might think that the growth of this inner nucleus of the personality would grow as a tree does, always growing another ring. You could imagine that someone might draw a mandala in one way and then later differentiate it in some way, but that is not true. In general the dreams show that this is not directed by conscious tendency, but is always completely broken up and then rebuilt. It is as if nature produced a pattern of wholeness and destroyed it again to produce a more differentiated pattern.[168]

The combination of mandala and floor is highly significant. The floor is the thing donna Soledad stands on, her standpoint, the basis of her world, and its construction is the symbolic reorganization of her life "from the ground up." This motif is common and occurs in dreams as a symbolic floor plan of a house or as a mandala designed in tile, fabric or wood at the center of a room. And the motif occurs in cultures where rugs are woven with a specific pattern that has a spiritual significance symbolic of the basis for one's best attempt at life. We see the same idea appearing also among the Pueblo Indians of the Southwest where mandala-shaped sand paintings are used in healing.[169] The sand painting creates a particular order and meaning that has a healing function for the participants in the ritual, just as donna Soledad is revitalized and centered by the lines of her floor.

Don Juan's Design

Don Juan's hand was involved in everything that happened between donna Soledad and Carlos. He groomed donna Soledad carefully for the confrontation, and at his request the "little sisters" aided her preparations. Don Genaro's apprentices knew about this test for Carlos and donna Soledad. They were even told of the possible outcomes and consequences. Don Juan told them that in the unlikely chance that Carlos did survive, they should trust him and allow him to lead them.

Everyone has foreknowledge of the battle except Carlos. Donna Soledad, however, lacked one essential piece of information about Carlos. She knew nothing of his awesome side and was not expecting the appearance of his double. It appears, then, as though donna Soledad had been set up to lose. She was told that Carlos was an easy prey for women but not that his irrational strength would be likely to save him. Donna Soledad says, "One of us was supposed to die tonight, but I didn't know it was supposed to be me."[170] Her situation parallels the experience of Croesus with the Delphic oracle. When he asked the oracle whether or not he should undertake a campaign against Persia, he was told that if he "attacked the Persians, he would destroy a great empire."[171] The oracle proved true, but the great empire that was destroyed was his own.

Although it is a grave mistake for us as humans to deliberately try to arrange or interfere with another person's fate, it is a fact that unconscious factors do arrange just such confrontations as the one we witness here. The experience of such "arrangements" remains the same and just as meaningful, whether we call the moving force God, fate or an archetype. We feel "set up" to face ourselves in ways we would least imagine or most wish to avoid. We shall look further now into the nature of this particular set up. Everyone's life has been changed by Carlos's arrival and by his victory. Though the changes are not immediately apparent, we do know that donna Soledad will go off on her own now and that the other apprentices are compelled to move and to move as a group. We shall look first of all at how don Juan's design affects donna Soledad and Carlos.

Donna Soledad believed that she needed something from Carlos, some "special power" that don Juan left with Carlos. The "special power" she sought seems to be just those aspects of Carlos that were responsible for his victory and her defeat: the irrational strength that appears when he is under pressure and also something of his "suicidal indifference," his willingness to take great risks. Donna Soledad's description of herself confirms this idea. She says that the problem she has on her journey is that she needs a "boost" since she is old, lacks courage and has "second thoughts and doubts." Carlos, on the other hand, is more connected to the awesome side of the unconscious through his use of power plants, and he may be able to give everyone a needed push. Donna Soledad is slightly older than Carlos and perhaps hesitant to challenge the last enemy of knowledge—the timidity and the desire for security characteristic of advancing age and of exhausted conscious attitudes. She needs to find in herself the recklessness she sees in Carlos; not the recklessness of making greater claims for power, but of accepting her vulnerability and the deeper mysteries of the unconscious. Carlos is the turning point in her life now, just as don Juan had been a turning point earlier. Don Juan taught donna Soledad to become a warrior and to experience herself more fully as a woman. Through him she was no longer able to conceal herself with mothering, with weight and with self-abasement. She has claimed power but claimed it too narrowly. Now the second man has appeared in her life, and I suspect that he will have an equally transforming effect upon her.

Prior to don Juan's entrance into her life, donna Soledad's adaptation to life was through the mode of the mother-martyr. Linda Leonard, a Jungian analyst in California, describes this pattern as one of four Amazonian modes of adaptation and defense, the other three being the Superstar, the Dutiful Daughter and the Warrior-Queen.[172] She says of the Martyr:

> Common to this pattern is the stoic self-denial which appears frequently in the areas of sexuality and creativity. In my view, this stems from a fear of the irrational and correlatively of the transrational. Fear closes this type of woman off from the joy and exuberance of life and from her own creativity and special vision.[173]

Donna Soledad tapped the heroic resources within herself and changed under the influence of don Juan, but there remains an aspect of defense in her strength, something that does not let her accept the irrational joys and sufferings of her spirit, her heart and her sex. With the breakdown of one's defenses, however, comes the opportunity to accept weaknesses, hurts and inabilities to function, along with one's creativity, love, passion and ecstatic experience.

As an example, consider the brief story told by Joan Halifax of

an Eskimo woman who experienced the shattering of her old ways—
in effect the cracking of her armor—followed by an awakening to a
new consciousness that could respond to the uncontrollable mystery
of life with joy rather than fear:

> Uvavnuk, a Netsilik Eskimo woman, achieved her great power in one
> extraordinarily dramatic instant. . . . a ball of fire came down from the
> sky and struck Uvavnuk senseless. When she regained consciousness,
> the spirit of light was within her. Her great power was used only to
> help her people. And when she sang, "all those present were loosed
> from their burden of sin and wrong; evil and deceit vanished as a
> speck of dust blown from the hand."[174]

Here is her extraordinary song:

> *The great sea has set me in motion*
> *Set me adrift,*
> *Moving me as the weed moves in a river.*
> *The arch of sky and mightiness of storms*
> *Have moved the spirit within me,*
> *Till I am carried away*
> *Trembling with joy.*[175]

Perhaps such a fate is awaiting donna Soledad.

When Carlos asks La Gorda why it is so important for donna
Soledad to overpower him, La Gorda's answer is, "Soledad is a
woman like myself."[176] She then says she will tell Carlos her story,
so he will understand. Her story is about being mistreated and
devalued by men; that is her answer to his question. Her life has
followed the pattern of a woman with an overly dominant, weak or
inadequate father, coupled with a mother's negative assumptions
about life such as, "One shouldn't expect much" or "Men are more
important than women." If donna Soledad is like La Gorda, then
the inner experience of self-respect has been missing, and she has
submitted to men who have not valued her. Through don Juan,
donna Soledad has seen her own depths and transformed the old
ways, but in the process she has also acquired new armor. She has
insisted on her own importance and strength, in order to compensate
the inner experience of weakness and of doubts about her value. In
this way donna Soledad shares the psychological profile of many
modern women who have worked at becoming as strong as they
imagine men to be, and then competing with men in a "masculine"
fashion. Thus, they often reproduce some of the rigidity that is
problematical in men. Such women cannot accept their vulnerability
or their special vision and are armored like their male counterparts.
The sensitivity shielded by armor needs to be reclaimed and the
armor softened, whether we are speaking of women or men.

We now need to look at the meaning of don Juan's design for

Carlos. We are told that he does not need anything from donna Soledad; however, there is obviously something for him to learn in the encounter. The trials are important for him in terms of what he must learn, not what he must take from others. The first thing he needs to learn is, once more, something about the nature of the devil's weed and the unconscious plots she spins. Inwardly, Carlos has to deny or rule out certain modes of behavior for himself, and outwardly, certain forms of relationship based on power. He needs to see the darker aspects of the unconscious in terms of the seductiveness of emotion and power as symbolized by donna Soledad. After all, throughout the first four books, we have seen Carlos's reasoning skills being unconsciously directed by his emotional needs for power and security. Again and again, he has reasoned and plotted to explain away, to control or to exploit his experience of knowledge.

The single most important purpose of the encounter for Carlos is to find a deeper relationship to the "Great Man" within himself. When the double emerges and saves Carlos from death, he realizes that he has unexpected resources and that he knows more than he is willing to admit to himself or to others. He has to live through this battle in order to receive donna Soledad's message:

> "The Nagual [don Juan] said that if I failed completely I should then give you his message," she said. "He told me to tell you that he had replaced your body a long time ago. You are himself now."
> ... "You are not your father's son anymore. You are the Nagual himself."[177]

Don Juan is gone, and there is no place for Carlos to turn but to his own resources. Anyone who has worked with a teacher and projected the archetype of wholeness onto that person, knows that ultimately it is necessary to withdraw the projection and take up the challenge of life alone. Some people experience a gradual, growing awareness of their inner strength and of the core archetypal factors fatefully shaping their lives. For others, these realizations may come in as sudden and dramatic a form as they do for Carlos. Carlos needs to know that the years spent in building a relationship to the unconscious have born fruit, that the relationship to the other side exists and endures independent of the presence of the teacher, and that the unconscious will support him.

Another aspect of the lesson is that it is not enough for him to understand; he must also assume responsibility in action for what he knows. His confrontation with donna Soledad is only the first occasion to realize more deeply his need to act; he continues to be tested, whether by the "little sisters" or by the unconscious, throughout the rest of the book. Seeing donna Soledad and himself in a new light, the old props are broken, and he now must relate to all of his companions as if for the first time. But he also sees his effect upon them and must take responsibility for that effect.

At the end of the book Carlos is faced with a choice, either to lead or to leave. The old ways and places have been destroyed, and where and how they all go depends on Carlos. For Carlos to assume such a role is for him to challenge his pattern of indulgence in wanting to understand but not act. For the others it is a different matter; perhaps Carlos has to make the choice and lead because he can offer a relationship to the outer world that none of the other apprentices has. La Gorda tells Carlos that while she is formless and a better sorcerer than Carlos, he knows the world of people better than she does. Perhaps Carlos needs the aid of his friends to live closer to the unconscious, and they need the bridge to the outer world which he can offer.

Women and the Wind

In the lull during the bouts of violence, donna Soledad tries to seduce Carlos with words. She explains to him the special relationship women have to the wind. There are four winds associated with the cardinal points of the compass, and each wind has different characteristics. Donna Soledad is on special terms with the north wind. The four winds are, as don Juan has explained to her, four goddesses. In other words, the winds constitute a feminine typology —different archetypal patterns for women.[178] Don Juan introduced donna Soledad to her specific wind because, he said, "women learn faster [than men] if they cling to their specific wind."[179]

What does it mean that women will travel faster on the path of knowledge if they find their individual wind? First of all, a woman's specific wind is the personification of her deepest instinct, her natural way, and a woman's pursuit of knowledge will flow more naturally if she listens to and follows her natural instinct. A woman will feel grounded, more secure than if she attempted to force her development in an artificial way. Consequently, she can begin to take greater risks on the path of knowledge.

Donna Soledad explains to Carlos how she was required to open herself to the wind. She was obliged to lie naked on top of a flat rock, and when the wind came she felt that it was alive. It licked her body and finally entered and moved around inside her. She thus internalized the experience of the wind, and in knowing the wind as an inner event she could listen to what it told her. The wind began to tell her what to do with her life and how to change. The wind, donna Soledad says, moves inside a woman's womb. If she is quiet and relaxed, the wind will pick her up. It will not only tell her what to do, but also provide the energy to accomplish things that seem beyond her grasp. Women, by virtue of their capacity to give birth, know more than men do (at least something different) about the secret of making things real. The archetypal force of the wind becomes an authentic experience when she feels its presence in her womb. The wind, for example, informs donna Soledad as she speaks that Carlos does not believe her when she tells him that the "little sisters" are don Juan's apprentices. It was also the north wind that enabled donna Soledad to transform herself from a tired old woman to a vigorous warrior.

The wind here is experienced as a feminine force, rather than masculine as it usually is in the Western Christian tradition. The wind as a goddess represents an archetypal feminine possibility of behavior and perception. To better understand a goddess as a "possibility," we can refer to the Greek goddesses. In Greece a woman could follow the goddess Athena by leading a cultured and intellectual life, advancing and fighting for the highest values of civilization without being called "mannish." Aphrodite represented an alternative, personifying a different archetype, a specific form of feminine sexuality and devotion to pleasure. Aphrodite was the one who broke boundaries, while on the other side we have Hera who saw herself always as wife and who was very much concerned with boundaries. Hera imagined fulfilment only through relationship to one man, Zeus, and consequently boundaries were important to her. Artemis on the other hand was a virginal goddess of nature, a huntress who shunned suitors.

If we imagine these familiar goddesses as "possibilities," as "winds" symbolizing natural trends of the feminine instinct, then we can come closer to understanding the experience described by donna Soledad. A woman could open herself (donna Soledad's image) to Athena and feel uplifted and carried by service to the sacred path the goddess personifies. Or a woman could be what many people refer to as "just a housewife" and yet experience exaltation and fulfillment in service to Hera. Similarly, a woman could come in touch with the divine spark within herself by following the ways of Aphrodite or Artemis—opposite trends but both sacred.

In the modern world we are lacking in symbols of what is deeply, instinctively feminine and holy. In other cultures women and men have been guided by feminine symbols in the form of goddesses. Both women and men could devote themselves to a particular goddess, and through that devotion find their own course, leading them naturally toward completion. Lacking these images, women today are likely to feel they have no support from cultural tradition and no sanction from above. Thus it is more difficult for them to grasp and respect what is trying to take shape within them.[180] The images we do have (housewife, career woman, mother, mistress and so on) are too narrowly shaped and lack spiritual and instinctual depth. As one woman's dream pointed out, "New times need new women."

The absence of collective images, however, offers the possibility of discovering new, more individual symbols. Donna Soledad's revelations suggest that we turn to the symbol-forming activity of the unconscious in order to find the sacred images attempting to be realized through us. The description of the north wind entering her womb suggests a process whereby an image is psychologically taken in. One then submits to the image and allows it to develop and to produce effects. The image is not analyzed and taken apart but is rather carried in such a way that it can affect our lives from inside out.

Toni Wolff, an analyst and coworker with Jung in Zurich, felt the need to have a typology specifically for women. A model of typology not only helps us to understand individual differences, but also to see more clearly our strengths and weaknesses. Jung's typology (extraverted and introverted feeling, thinking, intuition and sensation) is immensely valuable but does not serve the need for a specific typology for women. This is the void that Toni Wolff filled and the need that Linda Leonard is responding to in her work on the "wounded woman."[181] Although an awareness of one's particular and natural type is no substitute for the inner experience of the symbols of the unconscious, the awareness does lend understanding and clarity to one's behavior and to the feminine symbols produced in dreams and visions.

Because Toni Wolff's work is important to our theme and not widely known, I would like to describe her model in some detail. She represents the four structural forms of femininity along two axes, one personal and the other impersonal, as shown in the diagram on page 120. In this model the mother and the hetaira are at opposite poles of the same axis; both find their fulfillment in personal relationships but the mother responds to basic human needs whereas the hetaira responds to the unique individual interests of those around her. The medial woman and the amazon (her use of the term amazon differs from that of Linda Leonard, whose attention is focused on the amazon's armors or structures of defense) are both impersonally related to life, but the medial woman responds to the impersonal and archetypal factors of the inner world, while the amazon responds to the objective tasks of the outer world.

"Without condescension," the motherly woman "supports and consolidates what is unaccomplished and in need of help, and provides room for psychic development and greater security."[182] She will take up "motherly professions and activities" and in marriage strive to meet the emotional and practical needs of her husband and children. In relationship to a man she will protect and promote his needs for security, achievement and recognition; his social and economic position commands her attention more than his individuality. In marriage the motherly woman may ignore and suppress any feelings in her husband that would threaten the stability of the home; therefore, he may begin to feel like a "son or a necessary fixture" at home, and compensate for this feeling by exaggerating "his virility in his profession or in male company."[183] The negative aspect of the motherly woman shows up in anxious mothering, in the need to maintain relationships of dependency, and in the tendency to project her unrealized ambitions and her unacknowledged flaws onto the recipients of her care.

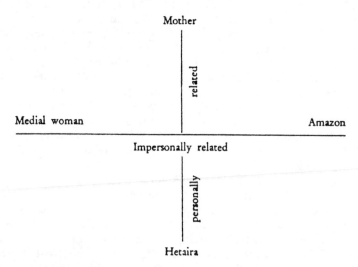

The hetaira relates as a companion and friend, and is intensely interested in her own and others' uniquely individual concerns, values and conflicts. Her natural tendency is "to awaken the individual psychic life" in others.[184] For her, social and financial security are unimportant in comparison to the "potentialities and nuances" of a valued relationship; consequently, she is in danger of harming herself and others by paying too little attention to the requirements of outer life. In love triangles the "other woman" is likely to be the hetaira. In marriage the hetaira runs the risk of repressing her needs for relationship with persons outside the family and, in compensation, making "secret lovers out of her sons and girl friends out of her daughters."[185]

Turning to the impersonal forms of the feminine, the amazon is independent, self-contained and directed toward achievement. "To be the wife of a distinguished man means nothing to her; she strives to win the laurels herself."[186] In relationship with a man she can be a "refreshing comrade . . . who makes no personal demands," who deserves respect and inspires achievement.[187] The negative aspects of the amazon are that she may be driven by "masculine protest," that she may repress personal conflicts in herself and in others and that she may measure relationships in terms of achievement or in terms of their business value.

Finally, the medial woman is described as an "agent," a "mediator" who is "immersed in the psychic atmosphere of her environment" and of her epoch. She expresses or acts "what 'is in the air,' what the environment cannot or will not admit, but what is nevertheless a part of it."[188] When she is capable of achieving personal definition and clarity, she may bring up and effectively relay to others the healing waters of the unconscious. When lacking personal definition, the medial woman may well activate unconscious material for which there is no container and thereby spread confusion; under such circumstances she may be experienced as "bewitching."

Toni Wolff suggests that a woman experiences one of these four feminine types as her natural tendency—what donna Soledad would call her "specific wind." By following her specific tendency, a woman will develop her personal talents, strengths and effectiveness more easily than if she were to force herself along one of the other paths. In time, however, she will need to develop the auxillary modes of perception and behavior, in order to fill out her personality. The opposite of her natural tendency remains the most stubborn and intractable function to deal with (as in Jung's typology) and should be considered the doorway to the unconscious. For example, under ideal conditions, the amazon would achieve personal satisfaction, confidence and security through her achievements in the outer world. In the meantime, additional growth would occur as she developed positive mothering qualities and a sensitivity to the nuances of individual relationships. The opposite structural form, the medial woman, represents "too great a contrast" to the amazon's character to be lived out concretely; and yet for the amazon, it would be through humbly turning inward to seek out the primordial images of the unconscious that she would arrive at the deepest experience of her totality and her personal myth. Similarly, as we have seen, donna Soledad's natural tendency had been to mother; hence the task in her individuation process involved integrating her medial and amazon qualities, and finally those associated with the hetaira, or individual relationship.

We will now examine the differences between men and women as they are described by donna Soledad, and look at the novel possibility that menstruation is more a blessing than a curse.

Menstruation: Door to the Other World

An animal fulfills its task in life naturally. A mountain lion is not likely to suffer confusion about whether it is really a jaguar or a rabbit. The mountain lion fulfills its task as a mountain lion, and the female and the male of the species each have their own inherent instinctive reactions and patterns of behavior. Women and men, however, seldom have such clarity about their sexual identities. We are all more or less confused about what is legitimately feminine and masculine, and in our understanding of our individual tasks. For us, there is both the biological task of the species and an individual task. A woman, for instance, has the task of being at ease with herself biologically in menstruation, sexuality, childbearing, child-rearing, menopause and also in the individual challenges of love and work. There is not, moreover, one mode of adaptation that alone is feminine. The possible paths at times oppose each other or oppose the collective values of the culture. Among these paths a woman needs to find the one that resonates with her as an individual. To complicate matters further, a woman is challenged to discover her own personal myth and, in addition, to realize the unconscious masculine aspects of her personality. No easy task and no surprise that we may consider the animals to be closer to God.

Donna Soledad, and later La Gorda, raise the issue of the differences between women and men. The issue is perhaps more difficult to resolve today, when there are equally strong tendencies to blur or discredit sexual differences and at the same time to heighten the awareness of sexual differences. In the previous section, we considered the images of the four goddesses of the four winds. This pointed to the possibility of experiencing different modes of feminine instinctual patterns as archetypal factors with a sacred foundation, rather than simply as modes of learned behavior which can also be unlearned. From this point of view, it is important for a woman to be at home in her natural tendency and to recognize that the natural way may be at variance with currently acceptable cultural images of what is feminine. Similarly, a man needs to be at home with himself first as a man and, in addition, to realize the ways in which his feminine soul image influences him.

To speculate on sexual differences, or on the differences between the feminine and masculine principles, is a tremendously valuable process so long as we are careful to grant our designations a good deal of relativity. For instance, in fairytales, our timeless documents of the collective psyche, the heroic task for a woman more often involves waiting and enduring isolation and suffering than setting out on an arduous and dangerous journey. The heroic course for a man is more often the difficult and dangerous journey. Now, this does not mean that women are never required to set out on a heroic journey for the "treasure hard to obtain," or that men may not have to wait and suffer in isolation. In fact, at certain times our own process of individuation will require us to withdraw these projections on what is masculine and what is feminine. While these two different tendencies may be collectively valid, they also may not in any way apply to a given individual. Therefore, the most reliable way of identifying one's natural masculinity or femininity, and of integrating the opposing sexual tendency in the unconscious, is the individual way of following one's unique process through the examination of the symbols produced by the unconscious in dreams and fantasies.

The difference between directly pursuing and openly waiting shows up also in donna Soledad's explanation to Carlos that men must leap into the abyss to claim knowledge, whereas women arrive naturally at the door to the other world every month through their menstrual cycle. Donna Soledad goes on to tell Carlos that don Juan believed women to be unequaled as sorcerers, that they commanded more power and that they learned more quickly than men. Donna Soledad disagreed with don Juan about women having more power, but that reaction can easily be seen as a reflection of her personal father complex, namely her tendency to give her authority away to men. The source of a woman's natural edge over men is menstruation. During her period, donna Soledad says, a woman becomes something else.[189] Menstruation brings a woman to the abyss, and there she may wait, ready to receive what the abyss produces.

During menstruation a woman's defenses against the unconscious tend to fall away, leaving her bare and open. For instance, during menstruation a woman may be more vulnerable, more sexual, more irritable, more introverted or more spiritual than she is at other times. The vulnerability, sexuality, irritability, introversion or spirituality is then the connection to the other side, the unconscious. In other words, during menstruation a woman may feel different but also more complete as her conscious experience is filled out by what has gone unattended, been repressed or never been conscious.[190]

One aspect of menstruation is its implication that a woman is not pregnant. If we look at menstruation in the way suggested by donna Soledad, then we could say that the temporary and literal barrenness lays a woman bare to be penetrated by the unconscious, to become pregnant with the psychological child, the new life of the spirit or soul within her. The monthly cycle then, is a periodic reminder of a woman's totality and of the new life in her that seeks to appear and to be contained. The new thing is ultimately the creative child, the hint of all that the future may hold. (This is true too of men, who dream of pregnancy and giving birth quite as often as women do.)

One example of menstruation as a symbolic opening to the inner world is a dream cited by Max Zeller in *The Dream—The Vision of the Night*. In the dream the woman goes to the bathroom and finds that her period has started earlier than usual:

> I see that sperms are among the blood. Later I check again and see that the sperms have developed and grown, which must mean that I am pregnant. The next time I check I find, instead of blood, drawings on the toilet tissue. They are drawings I had done years ago and had completely forgotten. They depict either an evolutionary process or the growth of a child to adulthood. It is the development of small stooped mankind to man in an upright posture. The last picture is that of a prehistoric woman holding the hand of a child. She is a lovely woman and wears just a loincloth. It reminds me of prehistoric man first discovering fire.[191]

The images that arise out of the menstrual blood are, donna Soledad would say, what awaits the woman who welcomes her monthly cycle as an occasion to receive and relate to her own unconscious.

Although the ancient menstrual taboo was the opportunity for a beneficial retreat to interior space for women, we may also assume that men had a hand in the taboo because of their fears and their experience of women during menstruation as somehow more over-powering, more awesome, more mysterious and more unpredictable. Curiously, there has been very little written about menstruation and even less in the way of scientific investigation—a significant fact in an age in which we investigate everything. It is not surprising that women are inclined to devalue and disregard what happens to them during menstruation, when there exists the common and insidious assumption that it is "Eve's curse."

The Stem, the Leaves, the Flowers and the Seeds

Assessing matters from Carlos's point of view, we can see in his experience of donna Soledad, the "little sisters" and La Gorda the fulfillment of what was anticipated in 1961, when he first learned of the devil's weed. We have seen the kinship between donna Soledad's drivenness and the roots of the devil's weed. The stem and leaves of the datura plant constitute the second "head" of the devil's weed and are used for curing illness. Lidia and Rosa heal Carlos's exhaustion and anxiety by taking him to don Juan's bed and sleeping on either side of him to protect him. They also prompt Carlos to heal the two wounds he has inflicted on donna Soledad and Rosa, and to learn that what wounds also heals. As a result of Lidia and Rosa, Carlos once again says "no" to the old way of disclaiming the need to act, and spontaneously discovers his own unsuspected resources.

The flowers of the datura plant are the third "head" of the devil's weed, used to make people crazy or obedient or to slay them. Enter now Josefina, crazy-making master of disguise. She was crazy when don Juan met her and she remains a bit crazy now. She feigns a psychological speech impairment while Lidia and Rosa seduce Carlos into an attempt to cure her. With the drama at its sentimental peak, Lidia and Rosa topple Carlos to the floor with Josefina clinging on top of him. Carlos can feel Josefina's heart not only beating against but entering his own chest, and then his nagual emerges once more. At this moment La Gorda opens the door and her entrance dissipates the frenzy of battle. Had Josefina been successful, the crazy rhythm of her heart would have merged with and possessed Carlos's own feeling. This process was, in fact, already occurring when Carlos was "obedient" to the sentimental appeals of the "little sisters."

The fourth "head" of the devil's weed, the seeds, is known as the "sober head," and of all the women warriors, La Gorda is indeed the sober one. Recall also that only the seeds of the devil's weed fortify the heart. La Gorda alone among these women has no interest in power and alone carries the goal of unifying and fortifying the members of this small community of warriors. She carries the seeds of the future, the seeds of potential for renewal and growth. The notion of being "one" was voiced to Carlos by donna Soledad and by the "little sisters"; it is voiced again by La Gorda but with a difference: she tells Carlos that they will one day be the same and that only the two of them can be the same.

Symbolically, Carlos has had to say "no" to the temptations of power, "no" to the inflation of being a healer (he can only touch the wounds he has experienced or caused) and "no" to the lure of eccentricity. He has yet to say "yes" completely to the seeds of knowledge—to an ethical commitment to the path of knowledge and to the life of the heart. Through his struggles, Carlos transcends the first three "heads" of the devil's weed and helps donna Soledad to sacrifice her preoccupation with power and control. He also helps the "little sisters" to sacrifice their closed and somewhat adolescent society and perhaps their limited identities as "curers" and "eccentrics." As he comes to a deeper experience of his manhood, therefore, he assists them to a deeper experience of their individual womanhood, and prepares for a higher level of relationship to himself and to others. This he is to learn from La Gorda.

Reclaiming One's Edge

La Gorda reveals to Carlos that the effect of having a child and of being a parent is the loss of one's completeness. She says we are complete before having a child and incomplete after having a child. She believes that the child carries an essential portion of oneself that has to be reclaimed; one must "steal the edge" back from one's child to be complete. This is a personal issue for Carlos because he has two children—a natural child he has never seen and his former wife's child by another marriage, a young boy to whom he is very attached emotionally. La Gorda thinks that the natural child has merged with his deep feelings for his stepson and that the two have become one.

There are essentially two psychological processes at work in La Gorda's insistence on the need to reclaim one's "edge" and to become complete. First of all, her story follows the pattern of Abraham and Isaac. La Gorda understands that one must sacrifice whatever one loves the most because it stands between oneself and God. No worldly attachment should come between the religious individual and God, and the love for one's child, as in the Abraham and Isaac story, is the supreme symbol of worldly human attachment. The other psychological process concerns the specific nature of what we project onto a child. We are incomplete when we project portions of our psychology onto any objects or persons in the environment, and since we invariably project the inner psychological child onto the physical child, to have a child results in being incomplete. The inner child is symbolically the spirit of renewal: the child is filled with potential and contains all that we might one day become. The child is also our spontaneity, our connection to the world of play, imagination and creativity. People dream of having a child when something new, fragile and full of potential is trying to enter consciousness. The symbol of the child is likely to appear whenever conscious-ness has become rigid, structured and settled. The archetype of the child is then behind the new and untried idea that would compen-sate the old age of one's conscious attitude.

If we look at what we are told about Carlos's relationship to his stepson, we can see how he is incomplete and what projection he needs to withdraw. The boy symbolizes friendship, laughter and the warmth of affection, and it is precisely in these areas that Carlos is blocked. The very mention of the little boy makes Carlos realize for the first time just how much he misses don Juan's presence and friendship. Carlos has not nourished his relationships. He ignored the "little sisters" for years, and with the Genaros his feeling of friendship took second place to his desire for their information. Carlos will retrieve his "edge" and become complete by learning to respect and love the company of the "little sisters" and the Genaros, not by "stealing" something from his stepson.

La Gorda tells Carlos that a boy will take the greatest part of his "edge" from his father and that similarly a girl will take it from her mother. It is just as common, however, for the child to take the greatest part of the "edge" from the parent of the opposite sex, that is, to be more influenced by the unconscious of that parent. The mother may, for instance, project her ambitions or her ambitious "edge" onto her son (a likely process in a patriarchal culture), just as the father may project the "edge" of his feeling onto his daughter. The other day I saw a mother and her son for an analytic hour. The mother was introverted and somewhat passive, whereas the son was active and frequently aggressive. I learned that her two daughters were also quite aggressive, as was her ex-husband. It seemed clear that this woman projected the "edge" of her aggression onto her children, as she had with her husband, and lived in a *participation mystique* with them. She could regain a portion of her completeness by becoming aware of her own unconscious aggression; and this in itself could lessen the internal pressure on the children to be aggres-sive.

La Gorda seems to think that a child loses its craziness when the parents' "edge" is reclaimed. She is correct about this to the extent that the child is acting out the parents' unlived life. But each child has its own craziness or "edge" that comes into being at birth, independent of the projections of the parents. The child's own indi-vidual "edge" may be quite enough and not require an additional burden from the parents.

As we have seen, balance and harmony are the warrior's way, and the need for balance stands behind the insistence that Carlos reclaim his "edge" from his stepson. Normally, when we become parents, we abandon the psychic child in ourselves in order to care for our physical child. In this way we split the parent-child pair and lose our balance; we indulge the responsibilities of our adulthood and the childishness of our children. To reclaim our balance we need to honor the claims of our inner symbolic child as well as the claims of adulthood.

Don Juan and Don Genaro Are Waiting

Carlos is about to leave the "little sisters" and the Genaros and return to Los Angeles. La Gorda tells him what he has been wanting to know from the beginning: the location of don Juan and don Genaro. Carlos knows that the two did not die and that they chose another vision to live in, but he does not know which vision. La Gorda reminds him of a red insect that don Juan pointed out to him in the mountains of northern Mexico. She tells Carlos that don Juan introduced all of the apprentices to those red insects and insisted that each hold the memory of the insect firmly in his or her mind. The world of those red insects is apparently a world of beauty and pleasure. That is the vision on which don Juan and don Genaro have focused their "second attention." It is the vision they are in and the vision in which all of the apprentices are to meet when they have fulfilled their individual tasks in life and developed their own "second attention."

If we take seriously the image of don Juan and don Genaro selecting the strange world of a red insect in the mountains of northern Mexico as the world in which their consciousness will continue, then the image deserves at least our wonder and our questions. If we look at the essential ingredients of La Gorda's statements, then to a point there is nothing surprising about them. Don Juan and don Genaro died and their spirits have simply gone to another world. Thus far there is no dissonance between what we are told and our own familiar Christian heritage that we have a spiritual body that ascends to heaven after death. Or we can say that the continuation of don Juan and don Genaro as a particular species of red insect is consonant with the ideas of reincarnation in the East. Here the agreements stop, particularly in terms of our Western tradition.

If the individual consciousnesses of both don Juan and don Genaro have left the world we know for another one, they have done so by virtue of their impeccability as warriors and their accomplishments along the path of knowledge. They have not done so by faith. In the Christian world view, the life of the spirit is guaranteed after death. In the world Castaneda presents, a continuation of consciousness after death is guaranteed only to the few who are able to develop the power of their "second attention" and the awareness of the double.

The other thing unique about the passing of don Juan and don Genaro is that they, as unique individuals, consciously selected the place where they intended to locate their consciousness after death. The location is highly specific, and furthermore, if we accept La Gorda's premises, it is a place that is available to any one of us who has the seriousness of intent to find out about those very specific red insects in the mountains of northern Mexico.

Many people can no longer accept the Christian articles of faith, and among these people it almost seems unfashionable to raise the issue of immortality, despite the fact that survival after death has been an urgent religious issue for humankind since the beginning of history. Immortality is the subject of the mystical tradition in all of the world's religions, past and present, and yet hardly ever do we hear anyone avow an interest in or concern with immortality. With the scientific revolution and with the weakening of traditional religious faiths, immortality as a legitimate interest has been put on the back shelf. Based on our history and our individual experience with death, it seems to me that the questions raised by don Juan's and don Genaro's unique departure are psychologically legitimate.

Healing the Split

As we have seen in *The Second Ring of Power,* the apprentices of don Juan and don Genaro are split among themselves. Don Genaro's apprentices get along fine among themselves, as do the "little sisters." When they are together, however, there is only strife and indulgence. No one wants to change. The split is between the ways of the two teachers, and it is also a split along sexual lines.

First of all I want to point out that don Juan and don Genaro are quite different individuals, and they have left their brands on their respective apprentices. We know that don Juan suffered terribly in his childhood, and perhaps for this reason it is no surprise to find that the apprentices of don Juan were all in bad shape, either physically or psychologically, before they became apprentices. In contrast, the apprentices of don Genaro were not "desperate people"; they were all managing well and were reasonably happy before their run-in with don Genaro. Another difference that stands out between the two men is that don Genaro encouraged his apprentices to live and not to worry about things, whereas, Pablito explains, the apprentices of don Juan were all taught not to enjoy but "to worry and try."[192] In fact, Pablito refers to impeccability as the warrior's ability to make himself miserable. Whatever differences existed between don Juan and don Genaro were bridged by the profound respect and love they had for each other.

This bridge breaks down when the two men of knowledge leave the world behind; the two groups of warriors are divided by mutual hostility. It is the task of these apprentices now to restore the harmony but to restore it in a new way. Previously, the center of their experience was concretized in two men; now it will be concretized in a man and a woman, Carlos and La Gorda, the two most impeccable warriors of the eight. The new level of harmony must unite the two paths of don Juan and don Genaro and also unite the two sexes. Thus the man-woman pair that now exists at the center of this small community anticipates a more differentiated aspect of psychological union. It is psychologically demanded of the carriers of the brand of don Juan to open themselves more to the experience of pleasure and ease, and to an authentic conviction about their own essential well-being and worthiness as individuals. It is also psychologically demanded of the Genaro apprentices that they learn to work and to try, even when they know that their work will change nothing. The Genaros also need to stay in touch with their own suffering rather than projecting it onto the "little sisters" and Carlos. In this way the split can begin to heal.

Don Juan and don Genaro told each of the apprentices that it was part of their sorcery task to stay together and to learn to live in harmony. As La Gorda points out later, the harmony envisioned is one in which all are accepted with no conditions and respected precisely as they are.

The other existing split among the apprentices is the division along sexual lines. The Second Ring of Power has delineated certain differences between the sexes. These differences need to be valued and respected; the differences, however, are not exclusively the possession of one sex or the other. For instance, these particular women, and women in general, may be more open to the unconscious than are men, and these particular men, and men in general, may relate to the unconscious in a more direct and focused way than do women. But any particular man or woman is not restricted to these general tendencies. There are times when men need to approach the unconscious with a receptive consciousness capable of taking things inside, and there are times when women need to make a dramatic, deliberate leap into the unknown. La Gorda confirms this when she says that the women can teach Carlos to contain his "second attention," and that Carlos will be able to teach them to push their "second attention."[193]

The withdrawal and integration of these teacher-related and sex-related projections will bring the apprentices closer to the harmony they are seeking. That is the work of consciousness, but consciousness alone cannot heal the wounds of these women and men warriors or the split in their community. Only the nagual, the unconscious, can touch the *source* of these wounds and heal them, and the movement of the nagual is dim, mysterious and unpredictable.

Conclusion

Before don Juan and don Genaro left us and this world they had one departing gesture with Carlos, Pablito and Nestor. Don Genaro stood several feet from the apprentices. Carlos saw a flash of light come from the ground and course through don Genaro's body. At this moment don Genaro performed a backward pirouette and weightlessly glided just above the ground as if to embrace the earth.

Don Juan explained to the apprentices that don Genaro loved the earth and that the earth in turn cared for him, sustained him and made his life complete and bountiful. "This is the predilection of two warriors," he said. "This earth, this world. For a warrior there can be no greater love." Don Juan caressed the ground and said, "This lovely being, which is alive to its last recesses and understands every feeling, soothed me, it cured me of my pains, and finally when I had fully understood my love for it, it taught me freedom."[194]

The love of the earth is the last lesson of don Juan and don Genaro in this world, and because it is the most difficult lesson, it seems appropriate to save this gesture of love for last.

Carlos has erased his personal history, disrupted his routines, assumed responsibility for the task he has in life, sought death as his adviser on the path of knowledge. He has cleaned the island of the tonal and become an impeccable warrior. Through active imagination he has wrestled with the allies of knowledge. He has dreamed the dream of the double and witnessed the vastness of the nagual. He even has an appointment with don Juan, don Genaro and the other apprentices in another vision. And yet Carlos has still not integrated the last lesson of don Juan and don Genaro: he has not yet learned to love the earth.

The earth is the soil under our feet, all things growing and living. It is the wind, the darkness, the change of seasons, the everyday world, our likes and dislikes, our friends and our enemies, the moments of vision and the moments of paying the bills. The earth is our fate. In this way we are all a bit like Carlos; we are not entirely sure that we want to live the life that fate has given us. This is the last lesson, the simplest and the most difficult.

Postscript

A week ago Carlos Castaneda's sixth book, *The Eagle's Gift,* became available. As anticipated, Carlos does abandon his reticence and begin to assume responsibility for his knowledge. Also, he and the other warriors drop some of their animosity toward each other, and bonds of respect and affection begin to emerge as they pursue the paths that the nagual reveals.

In *The Eagle's Gift* Castaneda richly amplifies the paths of stalking and *dreaming* and adds considerably to our understanding of these two approaches to the unconscious. Stalking and *dreaming* are, respectively, the ways of the hunter and the warrior discussed here in Chapters Two and Three.

There are major surprises in Castaneda's latest book. Briefly, la Gorda and the other warriors definitively leave their homes and their old clothes behind as they follow Carlos to Oaxaca, Mexico City and other locations. Their journey unlocks shocking memories that reveal the nature of their complex relationships, their unique tasks as warriors and the myth that stands behind don Juan's teachings, the myth they are called to live — the myth of the Eagle. Through the attempts to live this myth Castaneda offers us startling ideas about time, memory and perception and about the nature and purpose of consciousness.

Although the apparent coldness of the Eagle's design for humankind seems antithetical to the joy don Juan claims is the warrior's "ultimate accomplishment," we can hope that this is not Castaneda's final statement and that the attitude behind don Genaro's joyful embrace of the earth, and don Juan's caressing of the ground, will one day find a home in Carlos.

Boulder, Colorado
April 22, 1981

Notes

CW—*The Collected Works of C.G. Jung*

1. The only exception I know of is Dr. Arnold Mindell, a Jungian analyst who has lectured extensively on the don Juan material at the C.G. Jung Institute in Zurich.
2. "Symbols and the Interpretation of Dreams," *The Symbolic Life*, CW 18, par. 598.
3. Ibid., par. 601.
4. Ibid., par. 606.
5. I refer to the Native American spiritual tradition as though there were only one tradition when in fact there are many. Common features do exist among the many Native American cultures, however, and for this reason I will at times refer to the Native American tradition as something specific and singular.
6. "The Complications of American Psychology," *Civilization in Transition*, CW 10, pars. 946-980.
7. Ibid., pars. 978-979.
8. Richard de Mille, *Castaneda's Journey*, pp. 23ff.
9. Marie-Louise von Franz pointed out in Zurich in 1975, during a conversation, that if don Juan were fictional he would be a psychological complex. Since complexes are predictable and since don Juan is anything but predictable, she thought it unlikely that don Juan would be a fictional character.
10. Castaneda, *The Teachings of Don Juan*, pp. 13ff.
11. W.B. Yeats, "The Circus Animals' Desertion," in *The Collected Poems*, pp. 335-336:
    Now that my ladder's gone,
    I must lie down where all ladders start,
    In the foul rag-and-bone shop of the heart.
12. Castaneda, *A Separate Reality*, p. 16.
13. "The Problem of the Attitude-Type," *Two Essays on Analytical Psychology*, CW 7, par. 78.
14. Mircea Eliade, *Zalmoxis: The Vanishing God*, pp. 76ff.
15. Castaneda, *Tales of Power*, p. 230.
16. Castaneda, *The Teachings of Don Juan*, pp. 56ff.
17. "The Story of the Youth Who Went Forth to Learn What Fear Was," in *The Complete Grimm's Fairy Tales*, pp. 29-39.
18. Barbara Myerhoff, *Peyote Hunt*, p. 75.
19. Castaneda, *Journey to Ixtlan*, pp. 102ff.

20. Von Franz, *Shadow and Evil in Fairytales,* pp. 150-151.
21. Castaneda, *A Separate Reality,* p. 194.
22. Castaneda, *Journey to Ixtlan,* pp. 243ff.
23. Castaneda, *The Teachings of Don Juan,* p. 76.
24. Castaneda, *The Second Ring of Power,* pp. 282ff.
25. "It is characteristic of the Westerner that, for purposes of knowledge, he has split apart the physical and the spiritual sides of life, but these opposites lie together in the psyche, and psychology must recognize the fact."—C.G. Jung, in Richard Wilhelm (trans.), *The Secret of the Golden Flower,* p. 181 n.
26. "A Review of the Complex Theory," *The Structure and Dynamics of the Psyche,* CW 8, par. 201.
27. Ibid., par. 210.
28. Arnold Mindell, *The Dream Body.*
29. Castaneda, *Journey to Ixtlan,* pp. 75ff.
30. See Mircea Eliade, *Shamanism,* pp. 269-274 on the World Tree, and p. 273 for reference to the Tree Book of Fate.
31. Jung, *Memories, Dreams, Reflections,* pp. 44-45.
32. Ibid., p. 88.
33. Ibid., pp. 192-193.
34. Castaneda, *Journey to Ixtlan,* p. 164.
35. Joseph Campbell, *The Masks of God: Primitive Mythology,* p. 240.
36. Ibid., p. 241.
37. Ibid., p. 231.
38. Joan Halifax, *Shamanic Voices,* p. 52.
39. Joseph Campbell, *The Flight of the Wild Gander,* p. 159.
40. Ibid., pp. 159-163.
41. Ibid., p. 161.
42. "The Undiscovered Self," *Civilization in Transition,* CW 10, par. 540.
43. Campbell, *The Flight of the Wild Gander,* p. 189.
44. Frank Speck, *Naskapi,* p. 43.
45. Ibid.
46. Jung, *Memories, Dreams, Reflections,* p. 223.
47. Ibid., p. 225.
48. Von Franz, *Creation Myths,* p. 135.
49. Castaneda, *A Separate Reality,* pp. 260-262.
50. Hyemeyohsts Storm, *Seven Arrows,* pp. 6-7.
51. Jung, "Approaching the Unconscious," in *Man and His Symbols,* p. 57.
52. Ibid., p. 71.

53. Joseph Henderson, "Ancient Myths and Modern Man," ibid., p. 101.
54. My own translation.
55. See *Experimental Researches, CW* 2.
56. Castaneda, *Journey to Ixtlan,* pp. 83-95.
57. Cf. George Devereux quoting G. Fathauer: "It is necessary to stress in this connection that when a Mohave notices that one of the small whirlwinds, which occasionally arise in the desert, heads toward him, he immediately dodges it, lest it carry his soul to the land of the dead, causing him to die."—*Mohave Ethnopsychiatry and Suicide,* p. 181.
58. Jung, *Memories, Dreams, Reflections,* p. 264.
59. Naturally this would not be the case for someone who relied too heavily on the unconscious and avoided conscious deliberation.
60. Jung, *Memories, Dreams, Reflections,* p. 178.
61. Halifax, *Shamanic Voices,* p. 12.
62. Ibid., p. 11.
63. Ibid., p. 121.
64. Castaneda, *Journey to Ixtlan,* pp. 102ff.
65. See Jung, "The Spirit Mercurius," *Alchemical Studies, CW* 13, pars. 247-303.
66. Barbara Myerhoff, *Peyote Hunt,* p. 77.
67. Quoted by Jung in *Psychology and Alchemy, CW* 12, par. 548.
68. Myerhoff, *Peyote Hunt,* pp. 148-149.
69. Ibid.
70. Castaneda, *The Teachings of Don Juan,* pp. 21ff.
71. Castaneda, *A Separate Reality,* pp. 91ff.
72. "The Spirit Mercurius," *Alchemical Studies, CW* 13, par. 255.
73. Ibid., pars. 256-257.
74. Ibid., par. 267.
75. Ibid.
76. Ibid., par. 289.
77. Myerhoff, *Peyote Hunt,* p. 216.
78. Ibid., p. 217.
79. "The Spirit Mercurius," *Alchemical Studies, CW* 13, par. 276.
80. Castaneda, *The Teachings of Don Juan,* pp. 35ff.
81. "Paracelsus as a Spiritual Phenomenon," *Alchemical Studies, CW* 13, par. 222.
82. *Journey to Ixtlan,* pp. 207ff.
83. Von Franz, "The Process of Individuation," in *Man and His Symbols,* pp. 186-187.
84. Homer, *The Odyssey,* p. 210.
85. Jung, *Memories, Dreams, Reflections,* pp. 187-188.

86. Similarly, the alchemist, writes Jung, "extracts everything meaningful and valuable as in a process of distillation, and catches the precious drops of the *liquor Sophiae* in the ready beaker of his soul, where they 'open a window' for his understanding."—*Alchemical Studies*, CW 13, par. 222.

87. Castaneda, *The Teachings of Don Juan*, pp. 46ff.

88. Jung, *Memories, Dreams, Reflections*, p. 183.

89. Joseph Epes Brown, *The Sacred Pipe*, p. 21.

90. *Civilization in Transition*, CW 10, par. 554.

91. Castaneda, *The Teachings of Don Juan*, pp. 131ff.

92. Castaneda, *Tales of Power*, pp. 241-242.

93. Castaneda, *A Separate Reality*, p. 35.

94. Adolf Guggenbuhl-Craig, *Power in the Helping Professions*, p. 39.

95. Eliade, *Shamanism*, p. 152.

96. Von Franz, "The Process of Individuation," in *Man and His Symbols*, p. 234.

97. Eliade, *Shamanism*, p. 159.

98. "The Spirit Mercurius," *Alchemical Studies*, CW 13, par. 287.

99. Ibid.

100. Jung, *Two Essays on Analytical Psychology*, CW 7, par. 365.

101. Ibid.

102. Myerhoff, *Peyote Hunt*, pp. 247-248.

103. "The Psychology of the Transference," *The Practice of Psychotherapy*, CW 16, par. 523.

104. *Journey to Ixtlan*, pp. 118ff.

105. *Letters*, vol. 1, p. 459. See also von Franz, *C.G. Jung: His Myth in Our Time*, p. 112, and Jung, *Mysterium Coniunctionis*, CW 14, pars. 706-707.

106. *Letters*, vol. 1, p. 460.

107. *The Odyssey*, p. 181.

108. Arnold Mindell, "The Golem," p. 111.

109. Ibid., pp.113-114.

110. Ibid., p. 113.

111. Von Franz, *C.G. Jung*, p. 119.

112. Castaneda, *A Separate Reality*, pp. 137ff.

113. Castaneda, *Tales of Power*, pp. 135ff.

114. Castaneda, *A Separate Reality*, pp. 165ff.

115. *A Separate Reality*, pp. 20ff.

116. Maud Oakes, *The Two Crosses of Todos Santos*, p. 183.

117. See Jung, "A Psychological View of Conscience," *Civilization in Transition,* CW 10, pars. 850-851: "When one is talking with somebody whose unconscious contents are 'constellated,' a parallel constellation arises in one's own unconscious. The same or a similar archetype is activated, and since one is less unconscious than the other person and has no reason for repression, one becomes increasingly aware of its feeling-tone.... The psychoid archetype has a tendency to behave as though it were not localized in one person but were active in the whole environment."

118. Von Franz, *A Psychological Interpretation of the Golden Ass,* p. XIII-15. See also von Franz, *On Divination and Synchronicity,* pp. 39ff.

119. Castaneda, *A Separate Reality,* pp. 157ff.

120. Castaneda, *The Second Ring of Power,* pp. 156ff.

121. *Mysterium Coniunctionis,* CW 14, par. 41.

122. Ibid., par. 180, n. 312.

123. Ibid., par. 36.

124. Wilhelm, *The Secret of the Golden Flower,* p. 23.

125. See the rain-maker story in *Mysterium Coniunctionis,* CW 14, par. 604, n. 211: "As an example of 'being in Tao' and its synchronistic accompaniments I will cite the story, told me by the late Richard Wilhelm, of the rain-maker of Kiaochau: There was a great drought where Wilhelm lived; for months there had not been a drop of rain and the situation became catastrophic. The Catholics made processions, the Protestants made prayers, and the Chinese burned joss-sticks and shot off guns to frighten away the demons of the drought, but with no result. Finally the Chinese said, 'We will fetch the rain-maker.' And from another province a dried up old man appeared. The only thing he asked for was a quiet little house somewhere, and there he locked himself in for three days. On the fourth day the clouds gathered and there was a great snow-storm at the time of the year when no snow was expected, an unusual amount, and the town was so full of rumours about the wonderful rain-maker that Wilhelm went to ask the man how he did it. In true European fashion he said: 'They call you the rain-maker, will you tell me how you made the snow?' And the little Chinese said: 'I did not make the snow, I am not responsible.' 'But what have you done these three days?' 'Oh, I can explain that. I come from another country where things are in order. Here they are out of order, they are not as they should be by the ordinance of heaven. Therefore the whole country is not in Tao, and I also am not in the natural order of things because I am in a disordered country. So I had to wait three days until I was back in Tao and then naturally the rain came.'"

126. Lao Tzu, *Tao Te Ching,* chap. 77, p. 139.

127. *A Separate Reality,* pp. 99ff.

128. Jung, "Psychological Commentary on Kundalini Yoga," p. 4.

129. Ibid., p. 5.

130. Ibid. Till Eulenspiegel is a legendary German folk-hero whose exploits illustrate the superior wit of the clever peasant, often under the guise of thick-headedness. The same archetypal motif appears in fairytales as the "Dummling" or youngest brother, whose very naiveté and childlike response to the unexpected eventually wins the princess or treasure.

131. Castaneda, *Tales of Power*, pp. 118ff.

132. Ibid., p. 139.

133. Jung, *Memories, Dreams, Reflections*, pp. 264ff.

134. Ibid., p. 265.

135. Ibid.

136. Ibid.

137. Daniel Brinton, *Nagualism*, p. 11.

138. Ibid., p. 12.

139. Ibid.

140. Ibid., p. 5.

141. Ibid., p. 21.

142. Ibid., p. 26.

143. We find the same concepts as the tonal and nagual in other cultures as well. For instance, in ancient Egypt an individual was considered to have two souls, the *ka* soul and the *ba* soul. The *ka* soul corresponds to the tonal and the *ba* soul to the nagual. The *ba* soul was the immortal part of the individual and was represented traditionally as a bird with a human head. In China the same two souls were conceptualized as the physical soul, *kuei*, and the *shin* soul, the one that ascends to the world of the spirit at the moment of death. The concept of the tonal and nagual is thus not an isolated phenomenon. Based on the evidence from other cultures we can say that there is an archetypal tendency to form such ideas. See von Franz, *Individuation in Fairytales*, pp. 13-14 and Jung, *The Visions Seminars*, p. 312.

144. Castaneda, *A Separate Reality*, pp. 222ff.

145. "The Psychological Foundations of Belief in Spirits," *The Structure and Dynamics of the Psyche*, CW 8, par. 573.

146. Ibid., par. 585.

147. Ibid., par. 587.

148. Castaneda, *The Second Ring of Power*, pp. 154ff.

149. William G. Roll, *The Poltergeist*, pp. 169ff.

150. Castaneda, *Tales of Power*, p. 35.

151. Carl Kerényi, *The Heroes of the Greeks*, pp. 45-46.

152. See Carl Kerényi, *Zeus and Hera*.

153. Dr. Mindell anticipated this identity between the ally and active imagination in his Zurich lectures long before the publication of *Tales of Power.*

154. Burr Cartwright Brundage, *The Fifth Sun,* p. 83.

155. Ibid., p. 82.

156. Ibid., p. 83.

157. See Jung, "Answer to Job," *Psychology and Religion,* CW 11.

158. Castaneda, *Tales of Power,* pp. 262-263.

159. Wilhelm, *Secret of the Golden Flower,* p. 25.

160. Ibid., p. 24.

161. Jung, *Memories, Dreams, Reflections,* p. 322.

162. Ibid., p. 323.

163. Ibid.

164. *The Second Ring of Power,* pp. 9ff.

165. Ibid., p. 119.

166. Ibid., pp. 9ff.

167. Ibid., p. 115.

168. Von Franz, *Individuation in Fairytales,* pp. 31-32.

169. See Donald Sandner, *Navaho Symbols of Healing.*

170. Castaneda, *The Second Ring of Power,* p. 67.

171. Herodotus, *The Histories,* pp. 32, 48.

172. Linda Leonard, "Puella Patterns."

173. Linda Leonard, "Amazon Armors," p. 123.

174. Halifax, *Shamanic Voices,* p. 13.

175. Ibid.

176. Castaneda, *The Second Ring of Power,* p. 126.

177. Ibid., p. 68.

178. Cf. Carl Lumholtz, *Unknown Mexico,* vol. 2, p. 94. Lumholtz refers to a Goddess of the Western Clouds among the Huichol Indians as being Aphrodite-like.

179. Castaneda, *The Second Ring of Power,* p. 45.

180. An interesting and valuable attempt to reconnect modern women with their feminine instinct and image patterns is Sylvia Brinton Perera, *Descent to the Goddess: A Way of Initiation for Women.* It examines the psychological significance of the goddess Inanna-Ishtar's descent to her dark "sister" in the underworld. See also Marion Woodman, *The Owl Was a Baker's Daughter: Obesity, Anorexia Nervosa, and the Repressed Feminine.*

181. Linda Leonard, "The Puella and the Perverted Old Man."

182. Toni Wolff, "Structural Forms of the Feminine Psyche," p. 4. For a more easily available outline and discussion of Toni Wolff's work see Irene Claremont de Castillejo, *Knowing Woman,* pp. 63ff.

186. Ibid.
187. Ibid., p. 8.
188. Ibid., p. 9.
189. Castaneda, *The Second Ring of Power,* p. 50.
190. For a fascinating, Jungian-oriented study of the psychology of menstruation, see Penelope Shuttle and Peter Redgrove, *The Wise Wound.* They have attempted to show that menstruation, rather than being a curse, is woman's untapped resource for the experience of the depths of the unconscious. Their investigation covers scientific, mythological, religious, historical and psychological perspectives on menstruation and supports donna Soledad's assertions.
191. Max Zeller, *The Dream—The Vision of the Night,* pp. 158-159.
192. Castaneda, *The Second Ring of Power,* p. 199.
193. Ibid., p. 312.
194. Castaneda, *Tales of Power,* pp. 284-286.

Glossary of Jungian Terms

Anima (Latin, "soul"). The unconscious, feminine side of a man's personality. She is personified in dreams by images of women ranging from prostitute and seductress to spiritual guide (Wisdom). She is the Eros principle, hence a man's anima development is reflected in how he relates to women. Identification with the anima can appear as moodiness, effeminacy, and oversensitivity.

Animus (Latin, "spirit"). The unconscious, masculine side of a woman's personality. He personifies the Logos principle. Identification with the animus can cause a woman to become rigid, opinionated, and argumentative. More positively, he is the inner man who acts as a bridge between the woman's ego and her own creative resources in the unconscious.

Archetypes. Irrepresentable in themselves, but their effects appear in consciousness as the archetypal images and ideas. These are collective universal patterns or motifs which come from the collective unconscious and are the basic content of religions, mythologies, legends, and fairytales. They emerge in individuals through dreams and visions.

Association. A spontaneous flow of interconnected thoughts and images around a specific idea, determined by unconscious connections.

Complex. An emotionally charged group of ideas or images. At the "center" of a complex is an archetype or archetypal image.

Constellate. Whenever there is a strong emotional reaction to a person or a situation, a complex has been constellated (activated).

Ego. The central complex in the field of consciousness. A strong ego can relate objectively to activated contents of the unconscious (i.e., other complexes), rather than identifying with them, which appears as a state of possession.

Feeling. One of the four psychic functions. It is a rational function which evaluates the worth of relationships and situations. Feeling must be distinguished from emotion, which is due to an activated complex.

Individuation. The conscious realization of one's unique psychological reality, including both strengths and limitations. It leads to the experience of the Self as the regulating center of the psyche.

Inflation. A state in which one has an unrealistically high or low (negative inflation) sense of identity. It indicates a regression of consciousness into unconsciousness, which typically happens when the ego takes too many unconscious contents upon itself and loses the faculty of discrimination.

143

Intuition. One of the four psychic functions. It is the irrational function which tells us the possibilities inherent in the present. In contrast to sensation (the function which perceives immediate reality through the physical senses) intution perceives via the unconscious, e.g., flashes of insight of unknown origin.

Participation mystique. A term derived from the anthropologist Lévy-Bruhl, denoting a primitive, psychological connection with objects, or between persons, resulting in a strong unconscious bond.

Persona (Latin, "actor's mask"). One's social role, derived from the expectations of society and early training. A strong ego relates to the outside world through a flexible persona; identification with a specific persona (doctor, scholar, artist, etc.) inhibits psychological development.

Projection. The process whereby an unconscious quality or characteristic of one's own is perceived and reacted to in an outer object or person. Projection of the anima or animus onto a real woman or man is experienced as falling in love. Frustrated expectations indicate the need to withdraw projections, in order to be able to relate to the reality of other people.

Puella aeternae (Latin, "eternal girl"). Indicates a certain type of woman who remains too long in adolescent psychology, generally associated with a strong unconscious attachment to the father. Her male counterpart is the **puer aeternus,** an "eternal youth" with a corresponding tie to the mother.

Self. The archetype of wholeness and the regulating center of the personality. It is experienced as a transpersonal power which transcends the ego, e.g., God.

Shadow. An unconscious part of the personality characterized by traits and attitudes which the conscious ego tends to reject. It is personified in dreams by persons of the same sex as the dreamer.

Symbol. The best possible expression for something essentially unknown. Symbolic thinking is non-linear, right-brain oriented; it is complementary to logical, linear, left-brain thinking.

Transcendent function. The reconciling "third" which emerges from the unconscious (in the form of a symbol or a new attitude) after the conflicting opposites have been consciously differentiated, and the tension between them held.

Transference and counter-transference. Particular cases of projection, commonly used to describe the unconscious, emotional bonds that arise between two persons in an analytic or therapeutic relationship.

Uroborus. The mythical snake or dragon that eats its own tail. It is a symbol both for individuation as a self-contained, circular process, and for narcissistic self-absorption.

Bibliography

Brinton, Daniel G. *Nagualism.*Philadelphia, 1894.

Brown, Joseph Epes. *The Sacred Pipe.* U. of Oklahoma Press, Norman, 1953.

Brown, Vinson. *Voices of Earth and Sky.* Stackpole Books, Harrisburg, 1974.

Brundage, Burr Cartwright. *The Fifth Sun.* U. of Texas Press, Austin, 1979.

Campbell, Joseph. *The Hero with a Thousand Faces* (Bollingen Series XVII). Princeton U.P., Princeton, 1968.

——. *The Flight of the Wild Gander.* The Viking Press, New York, 1969.

——. *The Masks of God: Primitive Mythology.* The Viking Press, New York, 1969.

Castaneda, Carlos. *The Teachings of Don Juan.* U. of California Press, Berkeley, 1968.

——. *A Separate Reality.* Simon and Schuster, New York, 1971.

——. *Journey to Ixtlan.* The Bodley Head, London, 1972.

——. *Tales of Power.* Simon and Schuster, New York, 1974.

——. *The Second Ring of Power.* Simon and Schuster, New York, 1977.

——. *The Eagle's Gift.* Simon and Schuster, New York, 1981.

Castillejo, Irene Claremont de. *Knowing Woman.* Harper Colophon, New York, 1973.

Devereux, George. *Mohave Ethnopsychiatry and Suicide.* Smithsonian Institution, Bureau of American Ethnology, Bulletin 175, Washington, 1961.

Eliade, Mircea. *Shamanism* (Bollingen Series LXXVI). Princeton U.P., Princeton, 1964.

——. *Zalmoxis.* Trans. William Trask. U. of Chicago Press, Chicago, 1972.

Grimm, The Brothers. *The Complete Grimm's Fairy Tales.* Pantheon Books, New York, 1944.

Guggenbuhl-Craig, Adolf. *Power in the Helping Professions.* Spring Publications, Zurich, 1978.

Halifax, Joan. *Shamanic Voices.* E.P. Dutton, New York, 1979.

Henderson, Joseph L. "Ancient Myths and Modern Man," in *Man and His Symbols.* Ed. C.G. Jung. Dell, New York, 1964.

Herodotus. *The Histories.* Penguin Books, Baltimore, 1964.

Homer. *The Odyssey.* Trans. Robert Fitzgerald. Anchor Books, New York, 1963.

Jung, C.G. *The Collected Works* (Bollingen Series XX). 20 vols. Trans. R.F.C. Hull. Ed. H. Read, M. Fordham, G. Adler, Wm. McGuire. Princeton U.P., Princeton, 1953-1979.

———. *The Visions Seminars* (Notes of the Seminars, 1930-1934). Spring Publications, Zurich, 1976.

———. *Letters* (Bollingen Series XCV). 2 vols. Ed. Gerhard Adler and Aniela Jaffe. Princeton U.P., Princeton, 1973.

———. *Memories, Dreams, Reflections.* Ed. Aniela Jaffe. Vintage, New York, 1963.

———. "Psychological Commentary on Kundalini Yoga," in *Spring 1975.*

———, et. al. *Man and His Symbols.* Dell, New York, 1964.

Kerényi, C. *The Heroes of the Greeks.* Thames and Hudson, Southampton, 1959.

———. *Zeus and Hera.* Princeton U.P., Princeton, 1975.

Lao Tzu. *Tao Te Ching.* Penguin, Middlesex, 1963.

Leonard, Linda. "Puella Patterns," in *Psychological Perspectives,* vol. 9 (1978), no. 2.

———. "The Puella and the Perverted Old Man," in *Psychological Perspectives,* vol. 10 (1979), no. 1.

———. "Amazon Armors," in *Psychological Perspectives,* vol. 10 (1979), no. 2.

Lumholtz, Carl. *Unknown Mexico,* vol. 2. Scribner, New York, 1902.

Mille, Richard de. *Castaneda's Journey.* Capra, Santa Barbara, 1976.

———. *The Don Juan Papers.* Ross-Erikson, Santa Barbara, 1980.

Mindell, Arnold. "The Golem," in *Quadrant,* vol. 8 (1975), no. 2.

———. *Worlds in Collision.* Unpublished.

———. *The Dream Body.* Forthcoming.

Myerhoff, Barbara. *Peyote Hunt.* Cornell U.P., Ithaca, 1974.

Neihardt, John G. *Black Elk Speaks.* U. of Nebraska Press, Lincoln, 1961.

Noel, Daniel C., ed. *Seeing Castaneda.* G.P. Putnam's Sons, New York, 1976.

Oakes, Maud. *The Two Crosses of Todos Santos* (Bollingen Series XXVII). Princeton U.P., Princeton, 1951.

Perera, Sylvia Brinton. *Descent to the Goddess: A Way of Initiation for Women.* Inner City Books, Toronto, 1981.

Roll, William G. *The Poltergeist.* Nelson Doubleday, New York, 1972.

Sandner, Donald. *Navaho Symbols of Healing.* Harcourt, Brace, Jovanovitch, New York, 1979.

Shuttle, Penelope and Peter Redgrove. *The Wise Wound: Eve's Curse and Everywoman.* Richard Marek Publishers, New York, 1978.

Speck, Frank. *Naskapi.* U. of Oklahoma Press, Norman, 1935.

Storm, Hyemeyohsts. *Seven Arrows.* Harper and Row, New York, 1972.

Von Franz, Marie-Louise. *Creation Myths.* Spring Publications, Zurich, 1972.

————. *Shadow and Evil in Fairytales.* Spring Publications, Zurich, 1974.

————. *Individuation in Fairytales.* Spring Publications, Zurich, 1977.

————. *On Divination and Synchronicity: The Psychology of Meaningful Chance.* Inner City Books, Toronto, 1980.

————. *A Psychological Interpretation of the Golden Ass of Apuleius.* Spring Publications, Zurich, 1970.

————. *C.G. Jung: His Myth in Our Time.* Trans. Wm. H. Kennedy. Hodder & Stoughton, London, 1975.

————. *The Psychological Meaning of Redemption Motifs in Fairytales.* Inner City Books, Toronto, 1980.

————. "The Process of Individuation," in *Man and His Symbols.* Ed. C.G. Jung. Dell, New York, 1964.

Wilhelm, Richard, trans. *The Secret of the Golden Flower.* Causeway, New York, 1975.

Wolff, Toni. "Structural Forms of the Feminine Psyche." Herausgeber G.H. Graber, Bern, Switzerland, 1956.

Woodman, Marion. *The Owl Was a Baker's Daughter: Obesity, Anorexia Nervosa, and the Repressed Feminine.* Inner City Books, Toronto, 1980.

Yeats, W.B. *The Collected Poems.* Macmillan, New York, 1956.

Zeller, Max. *The Dream—The Vision of the Night.* Analytical Psychology Club and C.G. Jung Institute, Los Angeles, 1975.

Index

abandon, controlled, 22, 66
Abraham and Isaac, 126
accessible, being, 42-44, 63
active imagination, 22, 56, 67-70,
   93, 96-98, 100, 102, 112, 132
alchemy, 50-51, 66-67, 79
ally, 11, 55, 57-58, 81-82, 90-100,
   132
amazon, 114, 119-121
American psyche, 9-10
analysis, 7, 18, 26-27, 35-37, 43, 53,
   86, 90, 99
anima: 53-57
   definition, 143
animus: 53-55, 57
   definition, 143
archetypes: 38-40, 45, 47, 53-54, 80-
   81, 95, 98-99, 113, 116, 118,
   122, 127
   definition, 143
Argos, 78
Ashby, Allen, 45, 107
association: 40
   definition, 143
authority, inner, 8, 16, 106
average man, 21, 23-24
ayami, 46

ba soul, 140
balance, 29, 48, 66-67, 79, 81, 127-
   128
Benigno, 12, 18-19, 105
body, 10, 24-25, 75, 88, 96, 109,
   111, 116-117
Brinton, Daniel, 90
Brown, Joseph Epes, 59
Brundage, B.C., 98
Buffalo Calf Woman, 59

Campbell Joseph, 31-33, 38
Carlos: as chosen one, 17-18, 49,
   53, 63
   fiction of, 12-13
   interruption of apprenticeship,
   10, 16
   psychology of, 15-17
Castaneda, Carlos: as author, 7-1?
   107
   elusiveness of, 9
   a test for, 107
Castaneda's Journey, 12
Catalina, La, 61-63, 71, 108, 110
child, 126-128
Christ, 50-52
circumambulation, 41
community, 13, 106-107, 130-131
complex: 25, 35-36, 42, 55, 66
   archetypal, 98-99
   definition, 143
   exteriorized, 94-95
   negative mother, 40-41, 64
   routineness of, 36-41
constellate, 139
   definition, 143
controlled abandon, 22, 66
controlled folly, 81-83
coyote, 93, 95, 97-99
Creation Myths, 35
creative expression, 34-35
Croesus, 113
customs house, 89

Danae, 97
death, 29, 64-65, 69, 132
deer, magical, 47-48
de Mille, Richard, 12
devil, 16-17, 90, 105

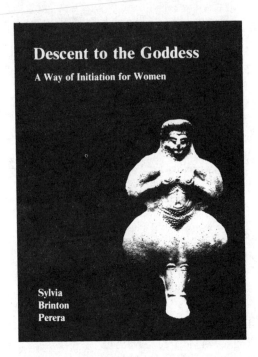

Descent to the Goddess

A Way of Initiation for Women

Sylvia
Brinton
Perera

6. Descent to the Goddess: A Way of Initiation for Women.
Sylvia Brinton Perera (New York). ISBN 0-919123-05-8. 112 pp.

A highly original and provocative book about women's freedom and the need for an inner, female authority in a masculine-oriented society.

Combining ancient texts and modern dreams, the author, a practising Jungian analyst, presents a way of feminine initiation. Inanna-Ishtar, Sumerian Goddess of Heaven and Earth, journeys into the underworld to Ereshkigal, her dark "sister," and returns. So modern women must descend from their old role-determined behavior into the depths of their instinct and image patterns, to find anew the Great Goddess and restore her values to modern culture.

Men too will be interested in this book, both for its revelations of women's essential nature and for its implications in terms of their own inner journey.

"The most significant contribution to an understanding of feminine psychology since Esther Harding's *The Way of All Women.*"—**Marion Woodman,** Jungian analyst and author of *Addiction to Perfection, The Pregnant Virgin* and *The Owl Was a Baker's Daughter.*

Addiction to Perfection

The Still Unravished Bride

A Psychological Study by
Marion Woodman

12. Addiction to Perfection: The Still Unravished Bride.
Marion Woodman (Toronto). ISBN 0-919123-11-2. 208 pp.

"This book is about taking the head off an evil witch." With these words Marion Woodman begins her spiral journey, a powerful and authoritative look at the psychology and attitudes of modern woman.

The witch is a Medusa or a Lady Macbeth, an archetypal pattern functioning autonomously in women, petrifying their spirit and inhibiting their development as free and creatively receptive individuals. Much of this, according to the author, is due to a cultural one-sidedness that favors patriarchal values—productivity, goal orientation, intellectual excellence, spiritual perfection, etc.—at the expense of more earthy, interpersonal values that have traditionally been recognized as the heart of the feminine.

Marion Woodman's first book, *The Owl Was a Baker's Daughter: Obesity, Anorexia Nervosa and the Repressed Feminine,* focused on the psychology of eating disorders and weight disturbances.

Here, with a broader perspective on the same general themes, she continues her remarkable exploration of women's mysteries through case material, dreams, literature and mythology, in food rituals, rape symbolism, Christianity, imagery in the body, sexuality, creativity and relationships.

"It is like finding the loose end in a knotted mass of thread. . . . What a relief! Somebody knows!"—**Elizabeth Strahan,** *Psychological Perspectives.*

Studies in Jungian Psychology
by Jungian Analysts

Quality Paperbacks

Prices and payment in $U.S. (in Canada, $Cdn)

19. Cultural Attitudes in Psychological Perspective
Joseph Henderson , M.D. (San Francisco). ISBN 0-919123-18-X. 128 pp. $15

20. The Vertical Labyrinth: Individuation in Jungian Psychology
Aldo Carotenuto (Rome). ISBN 0-919123-19-8. 144 pp. $16

21. The Pregnant Virgin: A Process of Psychological Transformation
Marion Woodman (Toronto). ISBN 0-919123-20-1. 208 pp. $18pb/$20hc

22. Encounter with the Self: A Jungian Commentary on William Blake's
Illustrations of the Book of Job
Edward F. Edinger (Los Angeles). ISBN 0-919123-21-X. 80 pp. $12

23. The Scapegoat Complex: Toward a Mythology of Shadow and Guilt
Sylvia Brinton Perera (New York). ISBN 0-919123-22-8. 128 pp. $15

**24. The Bible and the Psyche: Individuation Symbolism in the Old
Testament**   Edward F. Edinger (Los Angeles). ISBN 0-919123-23-6. 176 pp. $18

25. The Spiral Way: A Woman's Healing Journey
Aldo Carotenuto (Rome). ISBN 0-919123-24-4. 144 pp. $16

26. The Jungian Experience: Analysis and Individuation
James A. Hall, M.D. (Dallas). ISBN 0-919123-25-2. 176 pp. $18

27. Phallos: Sacred Image of the Masculine
Eugene Monick (Scranton/New York). ISBN 0-919123-26-0. 144 pp. $16

**28. The Christian Archetype: A Jungian Commentary on the Life of
Christ**   Edward F. Edinger (Los Angeles).   ISBN 0-919123-27-9. 144 pp. $16

29. Love, Celibacy and the Inner Marriage
John P. Dourley (Ottawa). ISBN 0-919123-28-7. 128 pp. $15

30. Touching: Body Therapy and Depth Psychology
Deldon Anne McNeely (Lynchburg, VA). ISBN 0-919123-29-5. 128 pp. $15

31. Personality Types: Jung's Model of Typology
Daryl Sharp (Toronto). ISBN 0-919123-30-9. 128 pp. $15

32. The Sacred Prostitute: Eternal Aspect of the Feminine
Nancy Qualls-Corbett (Birmingham). ISBN 0-919123-31-7. 176 pp. $18

33. When the Spirits Come Back
Janet O. Dallett (Seal Harbor, WA). ISBN 0-919123-32-5. 160 pp. $16

34. The Mother: Archetypal Image in Fairy Tales
Sibylle Birkhäuser-Oeri (Zurich). ISBN 0-919123-33-3. 176 pp. $18

35. The Survival Papers: Anatomy of a Midlife Crisis
Daryl Sharp (Toronto). ISBN 0-919123-34-1. 160 pp. $15

36. The Cassandra Complex: Living with Disbelief
Laurie Layton Schapira (New York). ISBN 0-919123-35-X. 160 pp. $16

37. Dear Gladys: The Survival Papers, Book 2
Daryl Sharp (Toronto). ISBN 0-919123-36-8.   144 pp. $15

38. The Phallic Quest: Priapus and Masculine Inflation
James Wyly (Chicago). ISBN 0-919123-37-6. 128 pp. $15

39. Acrobats of the Gods: Dance and Transformation
Joan Dexter Blackmer (Concord, MA). ISBN 0-919123-38-4. 128 pp. $15

40. Eros and Pathos: Shades of Love and Suffering
Aldo Carotenuto (Rome). ISBN 0-919123-39-2. 160 pp. $16

41. The Ravaged Bridegroom: Masculinity in Women
Marion Woodman (Toronto). ISBN 0-919123-42-2. 224 pp. $18

42. Liberating the Heart: Spirituality and Jungian Psychology
Lawrence W. Jaffe (Berkeley). ISBN 0-919123-43-0. 176 pp. $18

43. Goethe's *Faust:* Notes for a Jungian Commentary
Edward F. Edinger (Los Angeles). ISBN 0-919123-44-9. 112 pp. $15

44. The Dream Story
Donald Broadribb (Baker's Hill, Australia). ISBN 0-919123-45-7. 256 pp. $18

45. The Rainbow Serpent: Bridge to Consciousness
Robert L. Gardner (Toronto). ISBN 0-919123-46-5. 128 pp. $15

46. Circle of Care: Clinical Issues in Jugian Therapy
Warren Steinberg (New York). ISBN 0-919123-47-3. 160 pp. $16

47. Jung Lexicon: A Primer of Terms & Concepts
Daryl Sharp (Toronto). ISBN 0-919123-48-1. 160 pp. $16

48. Body and Soul: The Other Side of Illness
Albert Kreinheder (Los Angeles). ISBN 0-919123-49-X. 112 pp. $15

49. Animus Aeternus: Exploring the Inner Masculine
Deldon Anne McNeely (Lynchburg, VA). ISBN 0-919123-50-3. 192 pp. $18

50. Castration and Male Rage: The Phallic Wound
Eugene Monick (Scranton, PA). ISBN 0-919123-51-1. 144 pp. $16

51. Saturday's Child: Encounters with the Dark Gods
Janet O. Dallett (Seal Harbor, WA). ISBN 0-919123-52-X. 128 pp. $15

52. The Secret Lore of Gardening: Patterns of Male Intimacy
Graham Jackson (Toronto). ISBN 0-919123-53-8. 160 pp. $16

53. The Refiner's Fire: Memoirs of a German Girlhood
Sigrid R. McPherson (Los Angeles). ISBN 0-919123-54-6. 208 pp. $18

54. Transformation of the God-Image: Jung's *Answer to Job*
Edward F. Edinger (Los Angeles). ISBN 0-919123-55-4. 144 pp. $16

55. Getting to Know You: The Inside Out of Relationship
Daryl Sharp (Toronto). ISBN 0-919123-56-2. 128 pp. $15

56. A Strategy for a Loss of Faith: Jung's Proposal
John P. Dourley (Ottawa). ISBN 0-919123-57-0. 144 pp. $16

57. Close Relationships: Family, Friendship, Marriage
Eleanor Bertine (New York). ISBN 0-919123-58-9. 160 pp. $16

58. Conscious Femininity: Interviews with Marion Woodman
Introduction by Marion Woodman (Toronto). ISBN 0-919123-59-7. 160 pp. $16

59. The Middle Passage: From Misery to Meaning in Midlife
James Hollis (Linwood, NJ). ISBN 0-919123-60-0. 128 pp. $15

60. The Living Room Mysteries: Patterns of Male Intimacy, Book 2
Graham Jackson (Toronto). ISBN 0-919123-61-9. 144 pp. $16

Discounts: any 4-6 books, 10%; 7 books or more, 20%

Add Postage/Handling: 1-2 books, $2; 3-4 books, $4; 5-8 books, $7

INNER CITY BOOKS
Box 1271, Station Q, Toronto, ON, Canada M4T 2P4